D1094150

SITTING BULL
Champion of His People

Here is a swift-moving story of a courageous
Indian, hunted, cornered, driven from his own
land, and his epic battle for the rights of his
people. Sitting Bull displayed qualities of leadership when he was but a boy, and at an early age
became the leading spirit and chief of all the
Sioux bands. When the white man came, Sitting
Bull tried to save his people from the threat of
extinction. He was a great warrior in time of war,
a peaceful medicine man in time of peace. His
death is a grim story of a false arrest in the days
when there was no one to defend the Indian.

Chief Sitting Bull

Sitting Bull

Champion of His People

By SHANNON GARST

ILLUSTRATIONS BY ELTON C. FAX

JULIAN MESSNER

New York

Juv
E
99
D1
S605

BL/G

PUBLISHED SIMULTANEOUSLY IN THE UNITED STATES AND CANADA BY
JULIAN MESSNER, A DIVISION OF SIMON & SCHUSTER, INC.,

1 WEST 39 STREET, NEW YORK, N.Y. 10018. ALL RIGHTS RESERVED.

COPYRIGHT, ©, 1946 BY DORIS GARST

FIFTEENTH PRINTING, 1967

PRINTED IN THE UNITED STATES OF AMERICA

CALIFORNIA STATE COLLEGE
AT HAYWARD
LIBRARY

JT

TO MY SON
JOSEPH

BOOKS BY SHANNON GARST

Amelia Earhart: Heroine of the Skies
Annie Oakley
Big Foot Wallace of the Texas Rangers
Buffalo Bill
Chief Joseph of the Nez Perces
Cowboy-Artist: Charles M. Russell
Custer: Fighter of the Plains
Frontier Hero: Simon Kenton
Jack London: Magnet for Adventure
James Bowie and His Famous Knife
Kit Carson: Trail Blazer and Scout
Sitting Bull: Champion of His People
Three Conquistadors: Cortez, Coronado, Pizarro
Will Rogers: Immortal Cowboy
Broken-Hand Fitzpatrick: Greatest of Mountain Men

WITH WARREN GARST

Ernest Thompson Seton: Naturalist
Wild Bill Hickok

CONTENTS

SITTING BULL

Champion of His People

CHAPTER ONE

Boyhood of a Great Chief

A GROUP of Indian boys sat on a hillock watching the hunters ride off singing the buffalo song. Each hunter was leading his fleetest hunting pony. Each held his sturdy, painted bow, and his quiver of arrows hung just in back of his left arm. There was envy in the hearts of the watching boys. They longed for the time when they, too, could join in the buffalo hunt and do other brave and exciting things. Like the hunters, each lad had his bow and quiver of arrows, but their bows were small and their arrows had knobs at the ends instead of sharp points.

One of the boys nudged the companion nearest him.

"Look who rides alone at the rear of the hunters!" he cried. "Is it not Hunkeshnee?"

The other boys rose to their feet and peered closely.

Some of them were sure it was Hunkeshnee, the boy they called "Slow," a lad like themselves. Others were sure that it was a man; otherwise the *Akicita* (Indian police) would not allow him to go along.

They were, however, not long left in doubt, for the *Akicita* discovered his presence and made threatening motions with their rawhide quirts to send him back to camp.

A jeering wave of laughter from the group of boys greeted him as he rode up.

He grinned amiably, not at all embarrassed by their derisive hoots.

"Sometime they will let me go along," he said. "Now let us follow them to watch the kill. Then we will play the hunting game with the buffalo calves."

The Indian boys ran to loosen the hobbles on their ponies and gathered to follow Slow. It was their habit to follow him because from the time he was old enough to play games, most of which were in imitation of their elders' occupations, he was a leader—the one who suggested interesting things to do—the one who straightened out quarrels—the one whose calm self-confidence and good judgment inspired confidence in his companions.

At first he was called Jumping Badger; then, from his habit of always being deliberate in action and especially in speech, he was given the name of Hunkeshnee, Slow.

Now, in the year of Many Buffaloes, when he was twelve snows old, he was about to earn the name he would wear for the rest of his life and which he was to make world famous.

The boys rode slowly after the hunters, skirting the low hills so that they would not be seen by the wary *Akicita*, whose business it was to see that only full-fledged hunters were along and that none of the reckless young men dashed off ahead of the signal to spoil the hunt.

Suddenly the boys heard the bellowing of buffalo bulls and the hunting cry of the Indians. Their moccasined heels beat the ribs of their ponies. The hunt was on. They rode to the top of a hill and could see in the valley below the heaving waves of brown as the great herd stampeded toward the West in an effort to escape those stinging, death-dealing feathered sticks.

The herd and the hunters disappeared over a hillock but the boys remained on the hilltop, playing the game of who could shoot his blunt arrows the farthest, until the buffalo calves, frightened by the hunt into hiding, should finally venture forth. Then the boys would have their mock hunt, trying to hit the calves with their arrows as they ran, striking them with their hands in the Indian method of "counting coup" on the enemy.

Toward evening the hungry calves began to come from their hiding places and with wild whoops the boys were on their ponies, galloping to the chase, counting it an animal slain if one of their blunt arrows hit it.

Slow maddened one of the calves by hitting it at close range and with considerable force. At almost the same moment his galloping pony stepped into a prairie-dog hole and sent Slow hurtling over its head. The buffalo calf turned on the boy, snorting with rage. As the animal charged, Slow belied his name by the quickness of his motion in leaping to the beast's back. Seizing its ears in his strong hands he pulled with all his might until the hind quarters of the calf slowly, slowly sank until it was sitting on its haunches.

A mighty shout came from the throats of his companions. "He has conquered the buffalo calf!" they cried. "He made the buffalo sit down. His name shall be Sitting Bull."

Slow grinned at his friends. He released the ears of the animal.

"Watch me ride the buffalo calf!" he cried, pounding its ribs with his heels.

The young buffalo, crazed with fright, staggered to its feet and tried to shake off the unwelcome burden on its back. When that failed, it started to run, thundering over the prairie with the young Indian boy yelling and clinging to its back like the born rider that he was and with the pack of young savages in gleeful and noisy pursuit on their ponies.

This crazy ride continued until all of the participants were weary. Then the boy whose name from this time hence would be "Sitting Bull," slid from the broad back of the calf and scrambled behind Flying Hawk on his white pony.

When Jumping Bull heard of his only son's exploit he immediately sent the herald through the camp with word that there would be a feast that night in honor of the boy. Immediately his mother, Her Holy Door, and his oldest sister, Pretty Feather, and some of the women in neighboring tipis set great chunks of tender buffalo meat mixed with wild onions and other savory roots to boil by means of hot stones placed in water in pouches made of buffalo stomachs.

A big fire was set blazing in the center of the ring of Hunkpapa Sioux tipis and from all the lodges the Indians came filing to the feast, each arrayed in his best garments. Each carried his own cup or bowl made of the shell of a small turtle and his horn spoon. Each solemnly speared a hunk of meat with an arrow and went to seat himself cross-legged in the circle around the central fire. The chiefs, councilors and warriors were nearest the fire; the women and children formed the outermost circle. After everyone had eaten his fill, Jumping Bull rose to tell of how his only son conquered the buffalo calf.

"I now give him the name, Sitting Bull," he said. Then Sitting Bull was asked to rise and tell of the adventure. As he recounted his story the boys who were with him nodded their heads from time to time and shouted, "Hau! That is the way it was"—"I saw him"—"I was there"—in the manner of warriors testifying to the brave deeds of tribesmen.

Such telling of achievements was not considered boasting by the Indians. It was, rather, their method of keeping a record. Most of the activities of the tribes had for their main purpose the promotion of manly qualities in the young boys. Each phase in a man-child's development—the first word, the first step, the first animal brought down in the hunt, were duly celebrated by feasting and speech-making.

In such a manner, also, were the achievements of the braves made a matter of public record. It was the custom for each brave to stand up and tell of his brave deeds. This was called "counting coups." Of course, each coup had to be verified by someone who witnessed it. However, there was no lying among the Indians until they acquired this accomplishment from the white men.

An Indian rose to leadership or chieftainship through his qualities of bravery, quick thinking and daring. How were his people to judge of his qualities and accomplishments unless he told about them?

Young Sitting Bull told of his ride on the buffalo calf

quietly but with an amusing quirk to it because his sense of humor was always strong. This was the first time he had ever stood up to speak before grown men, but he did it with a quiet air of self-confidence that they liked and his amusing manner of speaking had them rocking with laughter from time to time.

When he finished talking he sat down and his uncle, Four Horns, rose to state solemnly that he knew from the first that his brother's only son, now called Sitting Bull, was destined for greatness. The night he was born the heavens were dark, but when his first wail, loud and strong as befitted a future leader, pierced the air, the full moon sailed in blazing glory from behind the clouds and an owl cried, "Hoo! Hoo!"

The firelight cast weird shadows on the faces of the Hunkpapa Sioux as they solemnly nodded their heads in agreement that these two omens presaged future greatness for Jumping Bull's son.

Four Horns then went on to tell of an incident which first displayed Slow's unusual fearlessness when he was but a baby of three summers.

When the Indians were on the trail they moved their belongings from place to place by means of the travois. This was an ingenious device made by attaching two lodge poles to the withers of a pony or the sides of a dog. Then a basket was formed by fastening a robe or hide between the poles. The young children rode from place to place in these crude but comfortable contrivances.

One day when camp was being moved, little Slow was riding in a travois attached to a dog. He was jouncing along, half asleep from the easy motion when a sudden jerk sent him wide awake and gripping the side poles with chubby fists. The dog had jumped a jack rabbit and was in hot pursuit, yipping and sending the travois to bouncing wildly. Her Holy Door screamed to see her baby being hurtled across the prairie. Other dogs joined in the chase, overturning travois and scattering the contents far and wide. Horsemen galloped in pursuit. When the runaway dog was finally stopped Slow was not frightened a bit. Indeed, he was laughing fit to split his little sides. When he got his breath he cried, "Fun! Fun! Slow want more fast ride."

The Hunkpapas in the circle agreed that this incident indeed showed that the boy was born with extreme fearlessness and was undoubtedly destined for greatness.

Jumping Bull then told of how he sometimes tried to frighten his son in the night by letting out a wild war whoop near his bed, but each time the boy sprang to his feet, seized his bow and arrow and was ready to battle any enemy. This was the usual practice of fathers in training their sons to be ready for emergencies.

Jumping Bull also told of sending the boy Slow after water at night when he was only eight snows old. Then he had Four Horns give the wolf howl and rustle the bushes, but the lad did not show fear.

After this recital of his son's qualities, Jumping Bull, who was considered wealthy among the Sioux because he owned many horses, rose to his feet and thanked his tribesmen for having attended the feast in honor of his boy. Then as the Hunkpapas stood up in preparation for the dance he moved among them quietly designating this one and that one to whom he was giving a pony on the morrow, for it was the Sioux custom to give presents on every occasion. To Sitting Bull he gave a strong bow and a quiver full of pointed arrows.

When the boy crawled between the buffalo robes in his father's lodge that night he was happy because of the honor that had been done him but he was in a serious mood, too, because so much was expected of him in the future. The responsibility lay on him like a heavy weight. He wondered if the carefree, adventurous days of his boyhood were over forever. Soon, however, sleep eased his cares from his mind.

The next morning, though, the serious mood still held his spirits in its grip. Taking the new bow and arrows his father had given him and snatching a piece of dried buffalo meat from the rack and his ever-present bow and arrow, he went out to the pony herd to whistle to his spotted pony —the one he had captured and broken himself. It raised its head from cropping the grass and whinnied in glad recognition. Sitting Bull loosened the rawhide hobbles, slipped on the bridle and leaped onto the pony's bare back and headed toward the hills. He wanted to be alone to think things over.

He urged the horse to an easy lope until he gained an eminence among the foothills, shut off by a fringe of trees. Then he dismounted, tied the hobbles on his pony and left him to graze while he clambered upon a boulder and stood with outstretched arms to greet the rising sun.

The habit of greeting the rising sun each morning was a custom among the Sioux. They always arose in time to step from their tipis, face the source of all life and stand for a moment of uplifted silence of spirit before plunging into the day's activities.

After greeting the rising sun Sitting Bull lay on a bed of

pine needles with his hands beneath his head and thought things over. Was he really to be great—a leader of his people, he wondered. It would be very fine to be a chief—to be admired and honored among men. To wear the head-dress of many eagle feathers. His father, Jumping Bull, was a great warrior but he was not a chief. If he, Sitting Bull, were ever to become a chief he must do it on his merit alone. The position would not come to him through heredity. Or perhaps he would be a shaman. Among the Sioux the Medicine Men were regarded with even greater honor than were the chiefs for they possessed supernatural powers.

The boy wondered if he perhaps might not be the possessor of some such supernatural powers, for it was true that he was able to talk with the bird people. Not everyone among the Hunkpapas was able to do this, he knew. Only a favored few were able to talk with the bird or animal people. It was a trick he had learned when a small boy.

One must be alone for the trick to work. Then it consisted simply of putting himself in complete harmony—of feeling strongly the sense of kinship with the bird people. Among the Indians, children of nature that they were, this feeling of kinship was not difficult for the more sensitive among them to acquire, for they were taught from babyhood that they were one with all the forces and things of nature. This was their religion.

He heard a rapid rat-a-tat-tat. He turned his head to follow the sound. It was his friend the gray woodpecker searching for his breakfast on the big oak tree. Perhaps the woodpecker would tell him his destiny.

He made himself very still within, then sent his spirit out to become one with that of the bird's.

"Tell me, friend," he whispered. "Am I to become a leader among my people?"

The bird cocked its head and turned beady eyes upon the

boy, then went racing around the trunk of the tree before he tapped out the message: "Rat-tat-tat—tat-tat-tat-tat, Rat-tat-tat-tat-tat-tat-tat-tat-tat-tat- tat."

And Sitting Bull knew he meant, "Yes, you will become

great. You will be great because you talk with bird people."

The boy smiled at this. He rose to his feet and stretched his arms.

"If I am to be great, little friend," he said, "I must be busy gathering coups so I will be honored among my people."

"Rat-tat-tat-tat-tat! Rat-tat-tat-tat-tat!" came a rapid, excited hammering and Sitting Bull recognized the warning, "Danger behind you!"

Automatically he gripped his bow and reached for an arrow at the same time as he whirled to see a grizzly bear lumbering to its feet.

The boy's heart froze. Here was a foe the Indian feared more than a human enemy. And he was alone. There was no one to depend upon. But he knew what to do. Not for nothing had he listened to tales around the campfire of those of his people who had faced this most deadly of foes. One swipe of that great paw and his life would be snuffed out like a smothered ember. He must not show fear. He must stand his ground, wait until the bear rose on its hind legs to strike, then send his arrow straight to the beast's heart. He must not miss. He would not have another chance. There would not be time to fit arrow to bow again.

With his feet far apart and his bow braced he stood waiting while the grizzly, with a roar of rage, rose to its hind legs, looming like a shaggy giant before him.

Then his arrow zinged from the bow, straight to its mark. The cry of the bear was almost human. It lunged forward a few steps, then fell and thrashed about for several moments, then lay silent.

Sitting Bull turned to the woodpecker.

"Thank you, little friend, for warning me," he said.

Calmly, then, he set about to cut off the bear's claws. Now he would be entitled to wear not only an eagle feather for this coup, but he would be allowed to wear that most cherished of treasures, the grizzly-bear claw necklace.

CHAPTER TWO

The First Buffalo Hunt

SITTING BULL'S first memories were of songs and
stories of valor. His mother sang to him of bravery
when he was a papoose hanging in his cradleboard from
her back or fastened to the side of her horse as they jogged
over the prairie at camp-changing times. Later, every evening by the fire in the center of their lodge his father told
of the heroism of the great men among the tribe. As soon
as he was able Sitting Bull was required to retell these
stories, for it was in this way that the history of the Sioux
was preserved, by handing it down from father to son.

At the numerous feasts around the big campfire in the

center of the circle of tipis the young Indian lad sat hugging his knees, his dark eyes sparkling with excitement while the hunters and warriors stood up in turn to tell of their deeds of bravery. Chills ran up and down the boy's spine as he listened. Time seemed to drag while he waited to become old enough to take part in the exciting doings of the young men.

The life of a Sioux boy, however, was full of excitement and pleasures.

There was the mouth-watering delight of the smell arising from a hide pot of stewing buffalo meat, or the oily, delicious taste of *Wasna*—ground meat mixed with wild berries and marrow. There was the excitement of moving camp when, amid barking dogs, chattering women and laughing braves, the boys leaped on their ponies and ran races. There were the quiet joys of hunting small game in the forests with bow and arrow. Every animal has its distinctive scent and Sitting Bull, like all Indian boys, early developed his sense of smell. He learned to observe and read signs. A turned blade of grass, a broken twig, a nervous bird, a bit of hair, an overturned stone, footprints, all told their story to alert young Sioux.

Sitting Bull soon acquired unusual skill with bow and arrow. He became an expert horseman and was on his pony so much that his legs became permanently bowed.

Then, of course, there were the exciting games. Indian boys lived a life of complete freedom. There was no school except the school of the universe. There were no chores for them to do. They were free to do as they pleased from morning until night. The only discipline that was exerted upon them came from their own desire to become like the men they admired and this discipline, that sprang from their own desire for achievement, was more effective than any force working from the outside.

In winter there was sliding on sleds made of buffalo ribs tied together with rawhide thongs or shooting bone disks across the ice to see who could send his the farthest. Most of the Indian games, however, were in imitation of the occupations of their elders. There was the snowball game with teams of equal numbers. Anyone who was hit was "dead" and out of the game. After this game the young braves counted coup on those they hit. *Che-hoo-hoo,* the Indian wrestling game, was a free-for-all in which equal sides engaged. There were numerous games of marksmanship with bow and arrow and a game similar to our hockey, called *Hu-ta-na-cu-te.* One end of a buffalo rib was whittled to a round point. The other end was squared off, the marrow cleaned out and two feathers inserted in the groove. The object was to throw this stick as far as possible over the ice. The boys played this game in freezing weather clothed only in a breechclout.

In summer there were foot or pony races and winter or summer a tug-of-war using a rawhide rope was popular, as was the game of follow the leader.

After young Sitting Bull's adventure with the buffalo calf and the slaying of the grizzly bear, Jumping Bull decided that it was time to equip his son like a man, since he seemed bent on engaging in a man's dangerous occupations.

"Son," he said, "the most important thing for a warrior to know is how to make a good bow. Come to the woods with me and I will show you how it is done."

Sitting Bull's heart leaped with pride to have his father treat him like a man.

As they walked through the forest Jumping Bull told the

boy about the different types of wood. Cedar, he said, made a strong bow, but was likely to crack. Willow bows were strong enough for boys to use, but now Sitting Bull must have a warrior's bow of ash, for he was strong for his age and could soon learn to use it.

Jumping Bull took great pains to select the best possible branch of wood for the purpose, then he cut it to the proper length and width, then showed Sitting Bull how to smooth it on a rough rock and bend it to shape over a small fire. After this the bow was polished until it was glossy and smooth. Then the back was covered with thin strips of wet sinew for extra strength.

When the sinews were thoroughly dried Sitting Bull himself decorated it with tassels of dyed horsehair and wavy red and black painted lines.

Then his father showed him how to make arrows of twigs of wild currant bushes. Each arrow had three feathers in the end.

There was not a prouder boy in the whole Lakota Nation than young Sitting Bull when he had his real warrior's bow and arrows. He looked with longing at his father's war paraphernalia that hung from his lance at the doorway of the tipi: at the war shield in its cover, at the painted parfleche holding the carefully folded war bonnet of eagle feathers, at the pictographs on the tipi depicting his father's deeds. He longed for these things, but they, too, must be earned. He must wait for an opportunity to win coups.

In the meantime he practiced ceaselessly with his new bow and arrows, acquiring skill and strength to use them.

When he wasn't practicing with his bow he worked at becoming an expert horseman, so that he could leap on his pony's back when it was going full speed, or could slide to one side, clinging only with one heel to a braided loop on the pony's neck.

Yes, being an Indian boy on the plains during young Sitting Bull's time was exciting, all right, but the lad who had already slain a grizzly bear was restless to become a real hunter and warrior. Childish, make-believe games no longer satisfied him. His restlessness grew to be almost unbearable during the time of the preparation for the ceremonial hunt during the moon when the buffalo bulls were fat. This hunt was for the main purpose of gathering hides, for at this time the hair was thin and easier to remove when the skins were cured.

Sitting Bull did not join his comrades in their rough, noisy games on the evening the hunt was being planned. He sat in the circle with his elders, watching the council tipi in the center of the ring. At last one of the old men emerged and summoned the messenger. Everyone sat tense and alert as the herald ran around pointing out the four braves who were to scout for the herd.

The firelight flickered on Sitting Bull's eager young face. "Oh, choose me! Choose me!" his heart cried.

But of course the herald passed by him. Brave Bear, Running Bull, Black Moon and Many Horses were chosen for the honor.

While the Indians in the circle rocked back and forth on their haunches singing praises of the young scouts, the four ran to their tents and emerged wearing only loincloths and moccasins and bearing bows and arrows. They ran around the fire twice, then dashed off into the darkness.

Daylight was just beginning to dissolve the curtain of night when an old man trotted around the camp calling "Co-o-o!" at each tipi. Every occupant leaped to his feet at this signal and almost instantly everything was excitement and commotion as the Indian women and children commenced pulling down lodge poles, rolling tipis and packing belongings ready to move camp.

As the sun was rising someone called out, "Hoppo! Here they come!"

A pile of buffalo chips had been heaped on a hilltop within sight of the camp. Brave Bear kicked the chips in four directions and a great shout arose from the camp. The buffalo had been found!

Then instantly the camp was silent while one of the councilors filled the calumet, puffed on it for a moment, then bent to touch it reverently to the ground, then to the sky and the four corners of the compass from whence all good things come.

"Have you glad news to tell us?" he asked Brave Bear.

"Hau!" Brave Bear answered. "A great herd is grazing quietly beyond the Hill of Tall Trees."

"Ha-ye-e-e! Ha-ye-e-e! Many thanks," the people cried.

Then the bustling recommenced while the tipi poles were tied to the sides of the ponies and the buffalo robes, horn bowls and spoons, stone tools and willow beds were packed and stowed on the travois or the ponies' backs.

Dogs barked. Young braves, gay in paint and feathers, leaped on their ponies. Boys galloped back and forth, kicking their ponies' ribs with moccasined heels. But young Sitting Bull did not gallop and shout with his friends. He sat quietly astride his pony and his face was serious. The usual holiday mood of camp moving and the hunt was not upon him today. He felt that he was too old for boyish actions, but he knew that his elders did not consider him old enough to take part in the hunt. Yet they should, he thought. Had he not slain one of the Grizzly Bear People, the arch—enemy of the Indian?

All day the Hunkpapas moved over the green prairies and rough hills. They traveled now in the order of march always used: The four old-man councilors went ahead. Behind them rode the subchiefs and some of the *Akicita*. Behind them came the people of the village and the travois, followed by the pony herds. At the sides and the rear rode more *Akicita* to keep order and to guard the people.

For two days they moved in this manner until the scouts gave the signal that they were as near the herd as they could get without frightening the bulls standing guard.

Quickly the camp was thrown up. The children were sent scrambling for rocks to hold down the edges of the tipis. The women and older boys erected the lodge poles while tipi covers flapped and magically fell into place until the circles of white cones stood in their accustomed places. In the center were the lodges of the chiefs and councilors and their families, while the outer ones stood like a protective ring with each door facing the direction of the rising sun.

While this was going on older women had been busy spinning round sticks between their palms, rotating the sticks over small boards until smoke came, then a tiny bead of fire that was carefully fanned and piled over with dry grass. Meanwhile children were busy bringing in parfleches of dry buffalo chips for fuel. In no time the camp was up and savory smells were rising from the bubbling kettles.

Usually all this caused great excitement and gladness in Sitting Bull's heart, but tonight dissatisfaction lay on his spirits like the huge stone beneath the thunder bird's nest.

Early the next morning all the dogs were tied to trees

so they would not disturb the hunt. The men got on their horses and rode silently to the top of the hill from which they could see the herd grazing in the valley below. The boys, too, were on their ponies, ready for the mock hunt of calves after the big animals had run away.

By now the bull lookouts had sensed the presence of the hunters and were pawing the ground.

Calves began to crowd their mothers. A wave of uneasiness swept through the herd and in a moment they began to mill and bellow. Now the signal was given and the hunters went racing lickety split toward the herd. But there was one hunter apart from the group. A slim, bronze figure on a mottled white pony. His mount was swift and used to racing. He put his ears back and stretched his neck and pounded on straight into the midst of the herd.

It was young Sitting Bull who could not resist joining the hunters. When he first found himself among that thundering herd a moment of fear gripped his heart. But only for a moment. Then the hot, strong smell of the shaggy beasts, the pounding hoofs, the stifling dust, the wild yells caused an overpowering wave of elation to sweep over him.

"Hi! Yi! Yi!" the shrill cry ripped from his throat.

He jerked arrow from quiver and fitted it to his bow and peered through the dust for a fat bull, galloped alongside it and let fly the arrow, aiming behind the shoulder blade. The animal snorted, dropped to its knees, then was up again and turned to charge the Indian boy.

Sitting Bull's knee gouged the pony's side, causing it to sidestep the charge of the furious, snorting beast while the boy quickly fitted another arrow to bow and let it fly. The buffalo's front legs buckled and its snout plowed the earth. Then with a groan it rolled over on its side, heaved a great sigh and lay motionless.

"Hi! Yi! Yi! Hi! Yi! Yi!" came shrill cries of triumph from Sitting Bull's throat. He had killed his first buffalo. Now no one could deny his right to go on the hunt.

Sitting Bull's uncle, Four Horns, came up and showed him how to butcher the animal, cutting it at the large joints so that the women could handle the meat, taking care not to cut the muscles so there would be large slabs for drying.

"The buffalo is our good friend," Four Horns said. "The *Wakan Tanka* sent him to give us not only our food but our tipi covers, our robes to sleep on, our clothes. His bones give us tools and weapons. His horns give us spoons. He even gives us material in his body to tan his own hide, and bones to make awls to pierce the hide and sinew from his back to sew with. Even his droppings we use as fuel for our fires."

"Hau!" agreed Sitting Bull. "The buffalo is the friend of the Sioux. Without him we could not exist. It was good of the *Wakan Tanka* to give his red children such a gift." When they finished butchering the great beast, he carefully set the skull to face the rising sun.

CHAPTER THREE

First Coup

OF ALL the days on the Sioux calendar Sitting Bull liked best the ones following the hunt. Then the hide kettle bubbled with savory meat, and various groups sat around the cooking fires gorging themselves until far into the night. Some thrust bits of meat on pointed sticks and toasted them over the coals, or wrapped them in leaves and thrust them under the embers.

This was always a time of dancing, singing and story-telling, when the hearts of all were content and full of thanksgiving to the *Wakan Tanka* for the gift to his red children of their brother the buffalo without which they could not exist. It was a time, too, when courtships flour-ished and many a young warrior left horses at some father's tipi and later held his blanket wide with one arm to wrap around a maiden in the marriage ceremony. But this sort of thing held little interest for the boy, Sitting Bull, at present. He kept his own eyes turned away from girls, as they did theirs from him, for Indian boys and girls did not mingle, even in play.

During the days following the hunt the camp was in a hubbub of activity. In practically no time the women erected racks on forked sticks and on these thin slabs of meat were drying. Squaws industriously pounded meat with chokecherries and marrow, making the *Wasna* to store in skins for winter use.

Horns were thrown in piles to be softened over heat and formed into ladles and spoons. Hoofs were boiled to extract the glue for fastening arrow points, and there was now an abundance of sinew for thread and bowstrings, as well as coarse hair to be woven into ornaments, ropes and belts. No wonder songs of gratitude bubbled to the lips of the Hunkpapas for the goodness of the *Wakan Tanka* in pro-viding them with the good things of life.

All of the after activities of the hunt fascinated young Sitting Bull, but there was one thing being done that was of intense personal significance to him now. His mother was tanning the skin of the buffalo bull he himself had killed. During his lifetime he had seen many buffalo and deerskin dressed but had never before paid much attention to the process because it had not seemed to concern him, but now he took a personal and intense interest in every step of the work. First Her Holy Door pegged the hide down on the ground, then with back-breaking labor fleshed the inner side by going over it with a gouge-like tool made of bone. Then she scraped the flesh with another sort of tool. Next she rubbed the hide with a mixture of the animal's own brains and liver. This substance was allowed to remain on overnight and was then rubbed in with smooth, flat stones and was afterward scraped to remove surplus brains and moisture.

Naturally Sitting Bull did not offer to help his mother with this task, even if it was his own buffalo hide—that was woman's work and any boy or man would be disgraced if he took a hand in it. He was, however, to take part in the things to be done with a portion of the hide—man things in which no woman could take a hand, for only men were allowed to make and handle the implements of war.

Already Jumping Bull had taken the part of the skin that came from the neck, the toughest part of the hide, and shrunk it while still wet over a fire built in a hole in the ground. When the tough circle of hide was dry Sitting Bull helped his father burn holes with hot sticks around the edge for the lashings to bind it to a strong circle of wood. When the shield was made, Jumping Bull retired to the sweat bath and to a night of fasting and prayer for a dream that would tell him the proper symbol to paint on his only son's shield. Although the shield in its present form was strong enough to turn an arrow or a lance, every Sioux knew that the real strength of a shield lay in its magic power. And always this power was gained through a dream in which the maker was told by some supernatural power what figure to paint.

When Jumping Bull returned from his dream he got busy with frayed-bone paintbrush and earthen paints and colored the body of the shield blue with a red circle around the edge and a black bird in the center. He fastened four black-tipped eagle feathers to the edge.

Sitting Bull was the happiest and proudest boy in the Hunkpapa camp that day as he went around showing everyone his fine war shield. Then he made a sturdy cover for it and hung it on a tripod facing the sun. Always when using the shield, his father told him, he must wear his hair in a knot like a horn on his forehead. This was according to the dream.

There was still a piece of the tough neck hide left and since Sitting Bull wanted a war club he went about to make himself one. And because he was a boy with imagination it was a war club such as none of the Hunkpapas had ever seen before. Most of them were satisfied with covering a pointed or egg-shaped rock with a piece of wet hide and fastening it tightly to a stout stick. But Sitting Bull's war club was shaped like a horse's head and had a sharp stick in the mouth, and skins dangling from the end. Her Holy Door was making him a shirt of the buffalo skin and long moccasins trimmed with elaborate porcupine quill embroidery.

Sitting Bull's father and mother were like the run of parents the world over. They were proud of their only son because he had already distinguished himself far above the average of Sioux boys his own age and they took pleasure in fixing him out in man things even as parents of today deck

boys out in Indian or Cowboy or Policeman suits. Some
day Sitting Bull would be a brave; in the meantime, he
could play at being one.

But the matter had gone beyond play with Sitting Bull.
His accomplishments so far only whetted his appetite for
still greater deeds—made him dream of the day when he
would have many coups to tell of around the campfire. Of
the day when he would be privileged to wear a trailing
headdress of many eagle feathers, each feather representing
a deed of outstanding bravery.

Because he had killed the grizzly and his first buffalo,
Sitting Bull was now allowed to take part in the men's
social affairs. It made him feel very important to join in
their dances and to sit around the fire listening to their
stories. He heard that his people, the Hunkpapas, once
lived across the Mud Water (Missouri River). Then the
Sioux had not been able to travel far and wide over the
plains as they did now because that was before they acquired
their big dogs (horses). Then they had only their dogs to
carry their belongings from place to place and because it
was harder to follow the buffalo herds on foot the Sioux
had to plant things in the ground for food and stay in the
same place until it was ready to eat. That sounded like a
dreary sort of existence to young Sitting Bull. He was glad
that his people crossed the Mud Water and traded for the
big dogs from Indians to the South* so that they could
roam the wide plains at will and follow the herds. He
would have hated to live in one place for many months.

He heard of the strange palefaced people he had never
seen. Their ways must be very queer. Elk Horn made the

* These horses were descendants of ones left behind by the exploring Spaniards
three centuries before.

Sioux around the campfire double up with laughter as he mimicked the strange beings who lived cooped up in ugly boxes and who covered themselves from head to toe in tight, uncomfortable clothes. Elk Horn wrapped himself in blankets after covering his face and chest with buffalo hair.

The Indians shuddered with disgust at such a spectacle. Themselves smooth-skinned, they considered hair on a man's face and chest repugnant and animal-like.

Elk Horn turned big toes out and walked with a combined waddle and strut in imitation of the white man. This made his audience roar with laughter. They knew that nature intended man to walk with toes straight ahead.

Then Elk Horn held his nose and shook his head as he tried to describe the strange odor of the palefaces. It was, he told them, as strong as that of the buffalo but not so pleasant.

Sitting Bull was agog with curiosity to see these strange, palefaced creatures Elk Horn was describing. They must be very miserable, inferior beings, indeed. However, they had curious and useful contrivances called thunder sticks that belched forth pebbles which brought death to whatever they hit. A few of the Hunkpapas had thunder guns. So valuable did they consider them that they were willing to trade many robes or ponies for their possession. Sitting Bull hoped that some day he would own one of the palefaces' curious thunder sticks.

The dreamer quality was always strong in Sitting Bull. But unlike many dreamers he had the force to put his dreams into effect. He had long dreamed of becoming a hunter. Now he had killed his first buffalo and so had become a hunter. Now his dreams were concerned with winning fame as a warrior, for it was the fighting braves who were honored and admired among the Sioux.

With the Plains Indians warfare was a matter of grim necessity—a constant battle for the possession of hunting grounds or for the purpose of revenge for injuries to their people. They fought not so much to destroy the enemy as for the purpose of gaining personal honors—of winning coups. These were gained by striking the enemy with a short coup stick or the hand and it was considered braver to strike a living than a dead Indian. According to the code of the Sioux, four warriors were entitled to strike coup on one fallen enemy. The first coup, however, or the greatest honor, entitling the winner to wear the coveted eagle feather, went to the first warrior to strike the enemy. Naturally it took more courage to be the first to count coup, for the enemy might be shamming and only waiting for a chance to rise and slay the daring Sioux who would collect his scalp, and it was often necessary to dash into the very midst of the enemy force to take first coup.

Many and thrilling were the dreams of young Sitting Bull's victories. No longer did the "pretend" games of his comrades interest him. He yearned now for the real thing, but, boy or man, he was never one to waste all his energy in merely wishing. He was the sort to put wishes into action. Already he was taking the first step by carving himself a short coup stick with the end decorated by tassels. Both the bone from which it was made and the hair tassel at the end were from the buffalo he had killed.

One night the Hunkpapa camp was attacked by Crows, the hereditary enemies of the Sioux. A number of horses were driven off and two Hunkpapas killed. Of course the

Sioux could not let this depredation go unpunished. Early the next day preparations were made for the return raiding party.

Sitting Bull watched the members of the war party set out on their ponies, each brave carrying his medicine bag to give him luck and leading his best horse that he would ride in battle. Jumping Bull was with the party.

When the braves were out of sight beyond the first hill, the boy grabbed his bow, slung his quiver of arrows over his shoulder, threw his shield over his left arm and dug his newly carved coup stick from beneath the buffalo robes on his bed where he had hidden it. Then he clambered on his pony and set out after the warriors.

The sun was in the middle when he came upon them dismounted behind a clump of bushes. They were busy stripping the covers from their shields and painting war designs on their faces and ponies. Then they put on their finest shirts and moccasins. Whenever there was time warriors always engaged in such preliminaries to battle because if they should be killed they wanted to be garbed in their best for their entrance to the Great Beyond.

Sitting Bull's heart was beating fast when he rode up to the group. What if they should laugh at him? What if his father should send him back?

Everyone stopped what he was doing and stared at the boy.

He rode up to his father and said manfully: "I have come to make war upon the Crows."

There was a silence that seemed unendurably long to Sitting Bull. If his father should order him back he felt that he could never endure the humiliation.

Jumping Bull's heart, however, was swelled with pride over the courage of this stripling son of his. It was difficult for him to speak.

"Do what is brave, my son," he finally said.

It did not take Sitting Bull long then to slip on his new buckskin shirt fringed with hair, to uncover his shield and to paint his face red; to place the imprint of his hand in red paint on his spotted pony's shoulder; to knot his hair on his forehead like a horn and leap to his pony's back.

No one laughed at the sight of his shield, coup stick and war paint. The Sioux were by nature a courteous people. By joining the party he had shown that his heart was strong. He would be given the chance to prove himself in battle. If he failed, then would be the time for ridicule.

The scout on a hilltop gave the signal that the approaching enemy was sighted.

"Hoka hey! Charge!" rang out the cry for attack.

"Ah—Ah—Ah!" The Sioux slapped their open mouths in the war cry.

"Ah—Ah—Ah!" came the shrill challenge from Sitting Bull's throat. His heels pounded his pony's sides.

The horse was fleet. In a short time he was up with the leaders, then ahead. The Crows, taken by surprise, and not knowing how many Sioux might be concealed behind the shrubbery, turned and galloped in the direction from which they had come.

"Hi! Yi! Yi!" Sitting Bull cried, plying heel and rawhide quirt to his spotted pony. He was gaining on the fleeing Crows and the distance between himself and his own comrades was widening.

The Indian in the rear of the Crow party heard the pounding hoofs of Sitting Bull's pony and cast a fearsome glance over his shoulder. He reined in his horse, fitted bow to arrow and aimed it at Sitting Bull's heart.

Instead of throwing himself to his pony's side, as he might well have been excused for doing, Sitting Bull continued to sit upright and raised his coup stick. With a clever swerve he dodged the death-dealing arrow and with a resounding crack brought his coup stick down on the enemy's head, knocking him from his horse, crying as he did so: "I, Sitting Bull, have conquered this enemy." This was so that there would be witnesses to his coup.

The other Sioux who came up made short work of the fellow, counting coups two, three and four.

It was a short battle. Obviously the Crows were in no mood for fighting. They had tangled with the Sioux before and they were on swift ponies now. Nevertheless, the Hunkpapas had a satisfactory number of coups.

After the fighting was over they gathered to talk over the exploits to which each warrior was entitled. Jumping Bull was grinning from ear to ear with pride over his son's bravery. Everyone had seen him take first coup that day. There was no dispute whatever over it.

It was night when they returned to the camp. With shrill yells of triumph they galloped to the center of the circle of tipis and rode around, each shouting at the top of his voice the deeds he had added to his record.

Sitting Bull's voice was not quite so loud. It quavered a bit as he cried: "I, Sitting Bull, took first coup today, striking an armed enemy."

A murmur of wonder sounded through the crowd at such bravery in a boy so young, and the eyes of his young friends were round with envy.

That night he joined in the victory dance, bending and

swaying, stomping and prancing to the beat of the drums and the wild, thrilling singing of his victorious people. His heart pounded with excitement. Never, never in all his adventure-packed life would he forget the heady triumph of his first victory dance when he of only fourteen snows was the hero of the occasion.

CHAPTER FOUR

The Vision Quest and the Sun Dance

JUMPING BULL decided that the time had come for his son to make the Vision Quest. Although only a boy in years he had proved himself a man at heart and hence mature enough to seek the Great Mystery.

Sitting Bull was sent with one of his father's best horses to smoke the pipe with Moon Dreamer, the shaman, and ask his guidance in preparation for the Quest.

For nearly a Moon Sitting Bull stayed in the shaman's tipi being prepared to go to meet the Great Mystery. The main purpose of this teaching was to keep the boy's thoughts on lofty things during his period of preparation.

Since the dream of his father, the shaman, and his own

heart was that the *Wakan Tanka* should make him a leader
of his people, Moon Dreamer's training lay along this line.
Although the boy learned much of the lore of Sioux around
the campfires, this knowledge was now reviewed and in-
tensified. He knew that the seven bands of Hunkpapas, his
own tribe, were part of the seven bands of Teton Sioux,
which were part of the seven great council fires of the
Lakota Nation. Dakota or Lakota means allied by a common language. The word Sioux is the ending of the word
Nadowessioux, an Algonquin word meaning snake or
enemies, but the Sioux called themselves Dakotas or La-
kotas, meaning "Allied" or "Many in one." The tribal divi-
sions were: Blackfeet, Brûlé, Hunkpapa, Miniconjou,
Ogalala, Sans Arc and Two-Kettle.

Moon Dreamer told him that the Dakotas were the
strongest, the bravest, the most finely developed of all of
the Indian Nations. In fact, they were The People, the
chosen of the *Wakan Tanka,* and he told several legends
to prove it. First, this fact was proved by the Sioux' possession of the sacred red-pipe country.

"There," Moon Dreamer said, "happened the birth of
the red pipe, which has blown its fumes of peace and war
to the remotest corners of the continent; which has visited
every warrior, has passed through its reddened stem the
oath of war. And here, also, the peace-breathing calumet
was born and fringed with eagle quills, which has shed
its quieting fumes over the land.

"The Great Spirit, at an ancient period, here called the
Indian Nations together and standing on a precipice of the
red-stone rock, broke a piece from its wall and made a huge
pipe, turning it in his hands, which he smoked over them,
and to the North, the South, the East and the West, and

told them that this stone was red—that it was their flesh—
that they must use it for their pipes of peace. At the last
whiff of his pipe his head went into a great cloud and the
whole surface of the rock for several miles was melted and
glazed.

"Once, many centuries ago, in the time of a great flood
that destroyed all the nations of the earth, all the tribes
of red men gathered on the Cotian du Prairie to get out
of the way of the waters, but it covered them in a great
mass and their flesh was changed into red-pipe stone.

"While they were drowning a young woman caught hold
of the foot of a very large bird that was flying over and was
carried to the top of a high cliff not far off, that was above
the water. Here she gave birth to twins and their father was
the war-eagle and her children have since peopled the
earth."

Sitting Bull sat silent when the shaman finished telling him
the legends. The firelight glowed on his intense young face
and his serious dark eyes. He had heard before of the red-
pipe land and of the medicine or leaping rock, a part of a
precipice that became separated from the main rock and
standing a distance from it much greater than the height
of the tallest man. Daring Sioux, wishing to prove their
strong hearts, leaped across, planted their arrows on the
narrow ledge across the chasm and leaped back again. The
bones of many who made the attempt lay at the bottom of
the chasm. Many others who planned to leap changed their
minds at the last moment when they saw the width of the
gap.

Sitting Bull resolved that he would join the next pilgrimage to the red-pipe land and would make the leap and
plant his arrows, but the arrows would be a special sort;

they would be feathered with eagle quills. For he was determined also to embark on another dangerous task: that
of catching an eagle to provide feathers for his war paraphernalia and for the feathers he could now wear in his
hair.

He was called from his reverie by the shaman's voice
droning on to tell him the legend of how the Dakota Nation
came into being.

"It happened in our sacred Black Hills country," he
said. "That is why the region is *Wakan* to us. It was in the
long ago when a solitary man awoke with the sun in his
eyes. Only his head was visible, for the rest of his body
was not yet formed; it was part of the ground. He gazed
about but saw no mountains, no forests, no rivers, nothing but soft mud, for the earth was still young. The man
struggled hard to drag himself slowly up until he was free
of the earth. At first his steps were weak and the soft earth
still dragged at his feet, but he kept his face to the sun
and it strengthened him and hardened the earth. Finally
he found he could run and leap like a free and joyous
creature. And from this man sprang the Dakota Nation.

"So you see," the shaman went on, "the earth is our
mother. That is why our hearts hold such an abiding love
for the earth and all of her creatures."

From *Wakan Tanka,* the Great Mystery, the boy learned,
came the life force that animated everything on the earth.
The same life force that had been breathed into the first
man flowed through the trees, the plants, the rocks, the animals—caused the sun to shine, the moon to glow, the stars
to twinkle, the wind to blow. The spirit of kinship must
become so real with him that he could speak with the
creatures of the forest in their own language.

"I can already speak with the bird people," Sitting Bull solemnly told the shaman.

Moon Dreamer nodded approvingly. "Then you may be one of the chosen ones," he said. "You may even become a Medicine Man. It depends on what power is given you when you seek the Great Mystery. Some seekers go through the ordeal and no vision comes to them. Those are the ones who are not great in spirit or strong in heart."

Sitting Bull's jaw became firm then as he determined to be strong in heart and great in spirit so that the Vision would come. He kept his thoughts good, ate sparingly and deeply felt his kinship with all things of the earth.

Then at last Moon Dreamer said the time had come for Sitting Bull to make the Quest. Together they rode far from the camp to the crest of a hill. Here Moon Dreamer dug a shallow hole and lined the rim with sacred sage. Then he placed curved willow poles over the hole and covered them with buffalo robes. Next he erected a pole in front of the sweat lodge and hung from it a bundle of sage, some feathers and a piece of red cloth. Then he built a fire and on it heated rocks which he rolled into the lodge. He bade Sitting Bull go in, then handed him ladles of water to dash over the hot stones. Sitting Bull sat in the steam until the perspiration was pouring from him.

At a signal from Moon Dreamer he dashed from the lodge and ran to the near-by stream and plunged into the icy water.

When he emerged rosy and shivering he went back to the hilltop and Moon Dreamer took the ponies and went back to the camp leaving Sitting Bull to remain alone, naked and unprotected, without food and water for three days and nights.

At night he lay inside the tiny lodge too miserable from hunger and thirst to do more than doze fitfully. He tried to keep his mind off thoughts of food and water and in a receptive attitude for the Vision, but it was a difficult task during the long, black hours, when his stomach was tied in knots and his tongue felt as big as a beaver's tail.

At the first streak of dawn he emerged from the lodge and stood before the little altar with arms outstretched and faced the rising sun.

"*Wakan Tanka,* open my mind and heart to wisdom," he prayed. "I am grateful for the good earth, for the sun that warms us, for the animal brothers and the life-giving waters. For all these I am thankful and for the tearing away of the veil that will show me the Great Mystery. I am thankful, *Wakan Tanka.*"

All day long he stood in this position, his face raised to the sun, turning slowly as it turned and seeking relief for his aching muscles on his couch of sweet-smelling sage only when the sun had gone to rest. But there was no relief from the tortures of hunger and thirst and the second night was worse than the first. And the second day and the third night and the third day the torture mounted steadily, almost too great to be borne. But still the Vision did not come. His heart began to despair. Was he going to be one to whom the Great Mystery did not reveal itself? Was he not to be one of the chosen ones? Were his dreams of greatness to go glimmering? He knew that no one to whom the Great Mystery had not revealed itself could rise to greatness among the Sioux. His medicine would not be good.

The sun had commenced to dip beneath the horizon on the third day and then the Vision came in a blaze of glory. There are no words to describe it. No man who has seen the Vision has ever been able to put it into words. It was like blazing light and wondrous music and a marvelous rising of the spirit all rolled into one. And for one dazzling, indescribable moment all things were clear to the boy. It was as though a gate had swung ajar showing for a brief moment some wonderful glimpse of greater things than were ever dreamed by man.

And then it was over. The sun had sunk and he was suddenly chilly and very weak. Yet a strange elation possessed his spirit. It had come. He had been in the presence of the Great Mystery for a brief but wonderful moment. He knew that he would never be quite the same again. Now he truly understood his kinship with all things of the earth. Everything was part of the great *Wakan Tanka*.

He seemed to be walking on air as he made his way back to the camp. Moon Dreamer came out to meet him and Sitting Bull joyfully told him of the Vision.

Moon Dreamer nodded approvingly. "You are one of the chosen," he said. "Your medicine is good. You will become a leader among your people so long as you do not forget you are one with *Wakan Tanka*."

The boy gratefully drank the soup his mother made for him. Then he sank back upon the buffalo robes to make ready for the next ordeal. Tomorrow he would take part in the Sun Dance, the final proof that he possessed the endurance and courage that would entitle him to honor among his people. Now that he had met the presence of the Great Mystery the ordeal of the Sun Dance held no terrors for him.

Already chosen braves had gone into the woods to select the sacred *Waga Can* or fleecy wood (cotton wood) . When it was stripped of branches, a crosspiece attached and erected in a circle of upstanding branches, it was called *Can Wakan* or "Holy Wood."

A figure of a man and one of a buffalo were tied to the crosspiece and a rawhide rope was attached. Then the drums began to beat and the people began to dance. Young Sitting Bull stepped calmly to the center of the ring and lay face down while the Medicine Man came forward to prepare him for the ceremony. With a stone knife he cut through the muscles of Sitting Bull's back beneath the shoulders, then ran the rawhide rope through the cuts and attached a buffalo skull to the rope; then he was pulled up and was to hang suspended until his weight tore away the muscles and released him.

With the blood streaming down his back, the boy raised his face to the sun and laughed and began the Sun Dance chant.

If he fainted or even gave way to his anguish he would be forever disgraced among his people and would be treated as a squaw for the rest of his life.

While Sitting Bull hung suspended, the other participants danced continuously, their faces raised toward the broiling sun. All day they must face the sun and pray for all good things—food, horses, victory in war—to come to the tribe.

There were those, however, who did not take part in the dance but who made it a point to ridicule the one who was going through the Sun Dance ordeal—to call him a woman, a coward—to assure him he was about to faint. Or they would sympathize with him and ask him if he did not wish to be cut down.

Sitting Bull, though, had a broad grin of derision for his tormentors.

"Hi! Yi! Yi!" he called. "I, Sitting Bull, laugh at pain. I have slain the grizzly bear, the buffalo, counted first coup on the enemy. Such a one does not faint from a little pain."

In spite of his brave words there were times when he thought he would faint from anguish. Times when the sun before his eyes was a burning blur and when his senses were on the verge of blotting out, but he summoned all his tremendous will power and made himself sing and kick his legs in time to the beat of the tom-tom. And at long last the tendons broke and he fell to the ground.

He rose to his feet and went to sit for a time beside his father. His parched body cried for water, but he could not drink or eat until the Sun Dance was over.

In a short time he was on his feet stamping and swaying around the circle with the rest, his face raised to the sun.

The watchers nodded and murmured their approval. Sitting Bull, although only a boy of fourteen snows, had proved himself of courageous spirit and already he had won honors that often took grown men many snows to acquire.

The next day Jumping Bull had a feast and gave away half his horses in honor of his brave and noble son.

CHAPTER FIVE

Every Day an Adventure

EVERY day on the great Plains was an adventure to Sitting Bull and his comrades. Indian boys were never at a loss for something to do. They hunted ducks, quail and young prairie chickens, wrapped them in mud and roasted them in slow fires. When the caked mud was removed the feathers came, too, leaving tender, juicy meat.

The boys caught fish by means of pony hair attached to a willow branch with a piece of meat tied to the end of the hair.

Sitting Bull's greatest joy, however, was horseback riding. A sense of elation filled his soul when he was on his fast spotted pony skimming over the grassy prairie with the sweet-smelling breeze against his face. He was thankful he had not lived in the days when his people did not have horses. Life must have been very dull in those days. Not only did the Indians have the joy of riding now and a much easier way of moving from place to place, but there were also the thrilling delights of horse stealing—a sport which the plains Indians had raised to an art. Young Sitting Bull himself had grown to be quite proficient in this dangerous skill. The Crows and Sioux made a habit of stealing horses from each other and nothing gave Sitting Bull as much of a thrill as to creep into a Crow camp on a dark night and cut the hobbles and steal ponies right from under the very noses of the sentries.

The Sioux, however, would not tolerate stealing among their own people. In fact, it was almost unknown. Sitting Bull could remember only one case of theft. A man stole a gun from a neighbor. The punishment for this crime was banishment from the tribe for one year. The forlorn culprit followed the band; his relatives carried food to him, but no one was allowed to visit with or speak to him. Even after he was re-admitted to the band, the disgrace hung over his head like a dark shadow. Lying and profanity were also unknown among the Sioux—until after their contact with the white man.

As Sitting Bull grew older, games of competition increased in importance with him and his comrades, and as he developed mentally and physically, so did his powers of leadership. There was a steadiness and dependability about him that inspired confidence in his judgment. He was often serious and quiet, but there was always an undercurrent of fun in his nature and he liked to play pranks. Although his leadership among the Hunkpapa boys was strong, he was not without rivals, the most threatening of whom was Gall, a tall, well-built and handsome lad whose daring equaled Sitting Bull's and whose self-confidence was second to no one's.

Gall had not won the honors Sitting Bull could boast, but he had a glib tongue and a way with him that brought followers to his side. The rivalry was a friendly one thus far, and neither boy dreamed that it would some day grow to deadly proportions.

Sitting Bull had long planned to catch an eagle. He told no one of his plans, for he liked to do dangerous things alone. Because of its majestic, solitary and mysterious nature the golden eagle was an object of veneration by the Sioux. Its wing bones were used as whistles to be carried by warriors or used in religious dances. Its talons were powerful charms, bringing "good medicine" to their wearer. The feathers were used in war bonnets, each feather denoting a coup. So highly valued were the golden-eagle feathers that a warrior would pay his best pony for a tail of twelve feathers.

Sitting Bull made his plans carefully. He kept his eyes open until he located the aerie of a great golden eagle. Early one morning he rode off from camp on his spotted pony, carrying his bow and arrows. He shot a jack rabbit and slung it across the pony, then he rode in the direction of the eagle's aerie. Soon he saw it sailing in the sky.

He grinned up at it and shouted: "Some day your fine tail feathers will trim the war bonnet of a great chief."

Finally he stopped the spotted pony, put the rawhide

hobbles on it and turned it to graze. Then he chose a place where some large rocks formed a natural pit. He covered the top with branches, sticks and leaves, placed the dead rabbit on top, then squeezed between the rocks and squatted down to wait, interminably, it seemed.

The sun climbed overhead, making Sitting Bull's hiding place the hottest spot in which he had ever been. Sweat poured from his pores. His thirst was almost unendurable. But still the golden eagle seemed to have no appetite for a dead rabbit.

The boy must have dozed. It was the rustling of the leaves over his head that aroused him. Quick as a thought his agile hands thrust through the branches and seized the eagle's legs. The cruel talons dug into his palms. He gritted his teeth from the pain but would not loose his hold. He jerked the great struggling bird down into the pit. Its strength was almost too much for Sitting Bull. One leg got away and the talons raked the boy's chest. The strong wings beat him. He thought the evil beak was about to peck his eyes out, but he pinned the struggling body down with his knee and got hold of the head and twisted with all his might until the huge body went limp.

As he crawled from the pit, dragging the eagle behind him, his knees almost buckled, he was so weakened from the struggle. But he managed to hoist the bird to his pony's back, pull himself up and ride to camp bearing the splendid trophy.

Jumping Bull was proud, but Her Holy Door wept when she saw the cruel gashes on her son's body.

"You should not go into such dangers," she wailed. "You are my only son."

"Would you have a son who sat by the tipi sewing moccasins?" Jumping Bull cried.

He searched out his finest porcupine-quill decorated hide sack for Sitting Bull to keep his precious eagle feathers in.

"Some day, my son, you will wear the finest war bonnet in the Lakota Nation," he predicted.

Soon after his adventure with the golden eagle Sitting Bull was given the opportunity he craved to make the pilgrimage of many sleeps to the sacred red-pipe land. No women went on this journey; it was a trek for brave hearts only and Sitting Bull was the youngest member of the party.

He took with him his shield, his strong bow and a quiver full of arrows feathered with the quills of the golden eagle he had slain with his bare hands.

It was amazing country as they approached the quarry, smooth, level and treeless with a vast expanse as far as eye could see of rolling green rising gradually to the cliff of red stone.

Sitting Bull listened patiently while the Medicine Man invoked the pipe-stone spirits the Sioux believed dwelt in the caves beneath the ledge. Then he clambered up the slippery sides, dug out a piece of the red-pipe stone with a sharp rock. Later, he would carefully fashion it into a sacred calumet. At present, however, he had something of immediate importance on his mind. He went over to look at the Medicine, or Leaping Rock, and his heart quailed at the sight. He did not see how any human being could leap across that chasm to the small column beyond. But it had been done. He could see the arrows sticking up in the rocks. And he knew there had been those who attempted the leap and failed. White Bear was along on this pilgrimage and was making a loud wailing for his son who three summers before had crashed to death on the crags below.

Sitting Bull's heart was pounding and his throat was dry. He wished now that he had not made his boasts to Gall that he would make the leap and plant his arrows. Now, suddenly, he wished he were back in the Hunkpapa camp smelling the savory stew bubbling in his mother's kettle. He had no urge whatever to make any reckless jumps. But he could not back out now. Since he had been foolish enough to brag ahead of time, he must make good his boast or be forever disgraced in the eyes of his comrades.

"*Wakan Tanka*," he sent up a silent prayer. "In the Vision Quest the Eagle spoke to me. Make me like the eagle—strong and fearless."

He stepped back, ran, then leaped, landed on the edge of the column across the chasm, stood for a moment on the slippery edge with his arms circling wildly to give him balance, then he was in the center of the column planting his eagle-tipped arrows.

There was not much room to get a running start on the column, but Sitting Bull was suddenly seized with a wild spirit of elation, as though he did indeed partake of the heart of the eagle. It was as though he still had momentum from his former leap and he made the return jump successfully.

Jumping Bull stood with bulging eyes and gaping mouth at this latest exploit of his daring son, but the other braves sang a chant of praise for the strong heart of Sitting Bull.

CHAPTER SIX

Changes on the Plains

TIMES were changing on the great Plains of the Sioux but at first the change was so imperceptible among the Hunkpapas that they scarcely noticed it. Jumping Bull told his son that before the time of his birth white men were unknown in the Indian country. Then the trappers came —palefaces who adopted the Indians' way of life. As a baby Sitting Bull had been taken along, bumping over the prairies in his travois, or in his cradleboard tied to his mother's back, to the annual fur-trader's rendezvous held each summer in the valley of the Green River. Here the Indians brought robes and hides and the trappers brought their year's catch and traded for various supplies brought in at this time by the fur companies. This was the way in which the Indians obtained vermilion, prized by the squaws for painting their faces; beads, mirrors, knives, various knicknacks and a few guns.

The boy, Sitting Bull, was to retain a faint, dreamlike memory of a certain history-making incident connected with a woman the like of which he had never seen. A woman who appeared to him all white and from whose throat came beautiful sounds. He did not know that this woman and the people she was with were in some manner tied up with his own destiny and that of his people. The fair-haired woman who entertained the trappers and Indians at the fur-trading rendezvous of 1835 was Narcissa Whitman, wife of a missionary leading a party to establish missions in the Nez Percé land in old Oregon country.

The most amazing thing to the Indians about this amazing party was the "rolling travois" (cart) Marcus Whitman was taking to the land of the Setting Sun.

To the most sensitive among the Sioux, the coming of the first white women and the first wheels to the Rocky Mountains caused a chill of apprehension to run up and down their spines.

They did not know it yet, but this same missionary, Marcus Whitman, was the following year to return to the States and guide the first caravan of settlers to the Setting Sun country, starting the first faint trickle that was finally to grow into a flood—a flood that would sweep the Sioux before it.

There were, however, a number of years of the good way of life left on the Plains. The only white men Sitting Bull knew as a boy were the occasional trappers who crossed his path. Men who lived like the red men and who were for the most part good of heart and who spoke with a straight tongue. Then there were the early traders, Picotte, Choteau, Primeau, Bordeaux and others with whom the Sioux had friendly dealings.

Life was still good in the land of the Dakotas while Sitting Bull was growing to manhood. There were exciting battles between teams of boys with mud balls stuck on the ends of willow sticks and flung with full force. A hit Indian was "dead" and coup could be counted on him.

They also painted their faces as if making ready for warfare and made attacks on bees' nests, "taking scalps" and holding a victory dance. The bees, however, were sometimes the victors in these battles.

Top spinning was also a favorite diversion. The tops were made of horn, bone, or wood carved heart-shape. They were spun by means of whipping them with a buckskin thong, the object of the game being to spin the top over or through various obstacles. The boy who kept his top spinning the longest was the winner.

The little girls played with wooden dolls dressed in buckskin or carried play papooses in cradleboards strapped to their backs.

Always there were the antics of the Thunder Dreamers, or *Heyokas* (clowns) to amuse both old and young. They painted their bodies and faces with zigzag stripes, depicting the lightning. It was their custom to do everything backwards: Their clothes were worn backwards; they mounted their ponies facing the tail; instead of entering a tipi through the doorway, they crawled underneath; they pretended to fire arrows at the enemy by firing at themselves; they fell to the ground if they weren't hit; they made motions of swimming on dry land and of walking on water; instead of taking off one moccasin and hopping across the stream on the bare foot, they removed one moccasin, then hopped across on the shod foot. But besides their business of providing fun, the *Heyokas* also had a serious function in the tribe, for they had good medicine with the sky powers and could bring on the rain or stop it at will.

From the Black Hills to the Big Horns the Sioux roamed at will, pursuing the buffalo, fighting and stealing horses for glory and honors. The brave who could creep into a hostile camp and make away with horses from under the very noses of the guards was a hero indeed. The Dakotas, of whom the Sioux were a division, were the most numerous, the bravest and the most splendidly developed mentally and physically of any of the tribes west of the Missouri River. Naturally, then, they were the rulers of the best hunting territory. When some enemy tribe invaded their domain, they drove them out and gained new coups.

Sitting Bull won his share of honors at horse stealing; indeed, it was his favorite sport. Although still a young man he was made a member of the Strong Hearts, one of the warrior societies. This entitled him to be a sash wearer. The sash was made of scarlet cloth trimmed with fur and dragging on the ground behind. Another insignia of the office was a close-fitting black cap covered with clipped feathers and bearing two buffalo horns worn over each ear.

Sitting Bull also bought a muzzle-loading gun, of which he was very proud.

One of Sitting Bull's horse-stealing expeditions he rated important enough for a place in the picture autobiography he later drew. A large party of Hunkpapas set out for the Crow camp one night. Sitting Bull was one of the four chosen to creep into the enemy village and drive off the horses. They were very successful and obtained a large number. They set out for their own camp driving the stolen animals as fast as possible.

At dawn the sound of pounding hoofs was heard. The Crows were coming hell-bent for revenge. A few of the Sioux were appointed as herders to press on with the spare animals; the others turned to face the on-coming Crows.

"Oo-waugh-waugh-waugh!" the shrill war cry resounded across the Plains as the painted Crows came charging.

Sitting Bull picked out the Crow chief for his own antagonist. He galloped forward then leaped from his horse and yelled, "Hi! Yi! Yi! I, Sitting Bull, would fight you. If you are not a woman, get off your horse and face me."

The Crow chief accepted the challenge. He slid from his horse. Sitting Bull crouched behind his shield and raised his rifle, but the Crow's gun belched fire first. Sitting Bull felt the bullet tear through his foot. Then his own rifle spoke and the Crow chief fell dead. Sitting Bull limped forward to count coup on the Crow he had killed. A few more shots were fired but the Crows lost heart when their chief fell and they turned and raced pell-mell back to their camp.

Sitting Bull was to bear the mark of this battle for the rest of his life. He would always walk with a slight limp.

At another time when the Hunkpapas were attacking a Crow band, one of the enemy entrenched himself in a deep ditch and was making considerable trouble for the Sioux. Already several had been slain, but it would never do to allow this man to escape and boast of the number of enemy he killed.

"Follow me!" Sitting Bull cried, galloping forward to make the charge. He struck at the Crow with his coup staff in order to make him rise and expose himself to the fire of his comrades.

The Crow, however, only grunted and poked his empty gun at Sitting Bull.

Seeing that the man had no more ammunition, Sitting Bull threw his own loaded gun to him and galloped back to his friends.

"I armed my foe," he cried, "for I would not see a brave man slain unarmed. Now I will take first coup for the eagle feather. Who will count second coup?"

Again he was galloping toward the ditch and this time his friends followed him. He took first feather, sure enough, but in so doing he was wounded—with his own gun!

For this deed he was made chief of the Strong Hearts. He was on his way to his steady rise to chieftainship over all the Sioux.

Under his leadership his people gained in horses, in guns, in fighting supremacy. Theirs by right of conquest were the choicest hunting grounds in the Indian country. He himself was a great hunter and his people were well fed, but they slaughtered animals only for their needs and they always apologized to the animal they killed, saying, "Brother, my family needs food. For this the *Wakan Tanka* made you."

And always they turned the skulls of the bison they killed to face the rising sun. The buffaloes who gave them life were sacred animals.

One day a party of Strong Hearts set out to wreak vengeance on the Assiniboin or Hohé Indians who had stolen some of their horses. Sitting Bull's black war horse became slightly lamed in this pursuit of the enemy and for once he was not in the lead. When he came up to the scene of activities he found the enemy had already been put to rout. The one victim who had not escaped, a boy of about eleven snows, stood with a defiant expression on his face, his blunt arrow fitted to his bow. The Sioux were about

to take the scalp of this boy but Sitting Bull came along, caught the boy up and swung him in front of him on his black horse.

"I will take the brave young Hohé as my brother," he said calmly. "He is too brave to die."

The Strong Hearts shouted their protest to this idea. They had no scalps over which to hold the victory dance. They felt cheated. But Sitting Bull was firm. He had a way of swaying others to his will. At last they grumblingly agreed to let Sitting Bull have the little Assiniboin as his brother. For this they never were sorry; little Assiniboin later became one of their famous warriors and was always steadfastly loyal and devoted to the man who saved his life. He had many chances to escape and join his own people but he chose to remain by the side of his "Big Brother."

It was not long after this event when the thing happened that brought sadness to Sitting Bull's heart.

The Hunkpapas were making way in a leisurely manner to their sacred hunting grounds in the Black Hills. As they were traveling, suddenly a whooping band of Crow braves in war paint darted from the forest.

Instantly all was confusion. Squaws and children screamed. Horses reared or attempted to run. Dogs barked. The Hunkpapas were taken off guard. Before they could collect their wits two of their own number had been killed before their eyes. It did not take long, however, for the Sioux to go into action and, though outnumbered, they soon had the Crows bested and ready to go home. But their chief was a brave man. He rode back and forth before the Hunkpapa line, firing his gun with devastating accuracy and shouting taunts.

Jumping Bull, Sitting Bull's father, started out after the brazen chief. His horse had been shot out from under him. He was afoot, but he showed no fear as he shouted: "If you are not a woman come and fight me. Loud words never killed anyone."

The Crow chief took the challenge. He slid from his horse and went to meet Jumping Bull. The Crow was brave all right. His gun was empty. He jerked out his knife as he stepped toward Jumping Bull. The Hunkpapa, seeing this, tossed aside his own muzzle-loader and reached for his knife—but it was gone! Probably it had slipped from its sheath during the melee.

With his bare hands the old man tried to grapple with his strong, young foe, but the Crow chief's knife found his heart.

Sitting Bull sprang forward to help his father but he was too late. An enemy arrow plowed through his shoulder but he did not even feel the pain. He saw his father's crumpled body lying on the ground and his heart grew furious with hate. He galloped after the fleeing Crow and slew him with his lance.

The Crows had enough fighting and galloped hastily home.

Sitting Bull loosened his hair and blackened his face and wailed loud and long in his grief for his father, and his mother and sisters and Little Assiniboin, his adopted brother, joined in the keening.

Sitting Bull wrapped his father's body in his best robes and placed it on a high scaffold near Cedar Creek. Beside him he placed his bow and arrow and war shield, also a parfleche of *Wasna*. He killed two of the old man's best horses and placed them beneath the scaffold so that Jumping Bull would be well supplied in the Great Beyond.

CHAPTER SEVEN

Gathering War Clouds

AS THE years passed Sitting Bull grew in power among his people. Not only was he brave in battle and outstanding in leadership—qualities that made him chief of the Hunkpapas, but it was also conceded that his "medicine was good," and so he became known also as a Medicine Man. This term is widely misunderstood by the white men. To the Dakotas the word *Wakan* (Medicine) meant both Mystery and Holiness and was used to designate anything sacred or of a mysterious or supernatural nature.

It was Sitting Bull's habit often to go to the hills by himself to commune with the Great Mystery. Frequently he had visions that enabled him to prophesy the future. It was said that he could call the buffalo herds when his people were hungry and his power to control the weather made him famous throughout all the Teton Sioux tribes.

There are those who scoff at such powers; none of the Indians today who were reared on the reservations possess these powers, but the old Indians who lived in the good days when their people were free are very positive that some of their leaders in the time when the red men lived close to nature and felt their kinship to all living things, possessed powers not exercised by civilized men.

Until the time of the trouble with the white men the function of a chief among the Sioux was mainly to be a sort of glorified father to his tribe; his discipline over them was negligible. In warfare it was every man for himself. So Sitting Bull had been mainly honored as a Medicine Man. With the encroachment of the white man, however, chieftainship among the Sioux took on new meaning.

Other tribes of the Sioux, the Brûlés, San Arcs, Ogalalas and Miniconjou came to smoke the pipe with the Hunkpapas and talk over the question of allowing the hundreds of white-topped wagons to continue to pass over the great Medicine Road.

"There is room for all," Sitting Bull said. "Leave the white men alone and they will not bother us."

"But their noise frightens away the game," spoke up Red Cloud of the Ogalalas.

Sitting Bull looked at him through narrowed eyes, studying him. He liked this young man, recognizing in him a power of greatness.

Finally Sitting Bull spoke, saying quietly, "Then we shall follow the game. Our best hunting grounds are in the Black Hills and the Big Horns. The white man's Medicine Road is far from there."

"The white man. Pfaugh!" Red Cloud spat out the words and there was a world of hatred in his tone. "They destroy everything they touch. Their smell alone is enough to chase away the game."

Sitting Bull himself had no love for the white man but in the beginning it was his policy to leave them alone in the hope that they in turn would leave his people alone. That was all he asked, but when, in the year the grasshoppers came, he saw the line of white-topped wagons stretch in a never-ending stream, he knew that eventually there would be trouble.

That summer the emigrants camping temporarily near Fort Laramie gave a big feast for the Sioux. The peace pipe was passed and speeches were made avowing friendly relations on both sides.

Later Colonel Stephen Kearny led five companies of dragoons over South Pass with the two-fold purpose of protecting the emigrants and impressing the Indians. Sitting Bull, seeing their shining carbines and their awe-inspiring wagon-guns (cannon) felt a cloud of dread envelop his spirits. Again and again he cautioned his people to let the white men alone. They, however, would not be prevented from attending the big meetings around Fort Laramie where feasts were held and many presents given away.

"Broken Hand" Fitzpatrick, a former trapper whom the Indians trusted, had been appointed agent—a good choice.

Colonel Kearny made arrangements for a general council for all tribes between the Fort and the Platte River. In the center of the council ground the Stars and Stripes were raised and a flag of Indian design bearing two bands said to represent the winds, with nine stars above the bands and clasped hands beneath.

The white men, always ignorant of Indian ways, made innumerable blunders. Kearny made one now. He said that instead of dealing with the chiefs of several Sioux tribes, he preferred to appoint one head of all the tribes and to deal with him. And he appointed such a "chief," Conquering Bear. This appointment of course meant nothing at all to the Sioux. Their chiefs earned the honor and they would continue to gather together in various bands and in various places. No "paper chief" could possibly have any influence over the entire Sioux Nation. However, they were agreeable and did nothing to disillusion Kearny, who, after the pipe had gone around, rose to make a speech. He told of the concern of the Great Father at Washington for his red children of the Plains. He told them that the emigrant road must be kept open.

Conquering Bear then made a fitting speech in reply, after which presents of red and green blankets, tobacco, knives, mirrors, beads and other trinkets were given away. Then the cannon was fired and as the shell burst a cry of amazement came from the throats of the Indians. They were sufficiently impressed by the power of the Blue Coats— for the time being.

In the next few years, however, Sitting Bull was hard put to hold his young warriors in line when, during the summers, the line of caravans stretched as far as eye could see and the game were driven farther and farther away and for miles along the Platte River Trail the grass was cropped to the ground by the emigrants' livestock.

When the Indians were hungry they considered it within their rights to go up to a caravan and demand food. Often this frightened the emigrants. Some of them were overly eager to shoot the "thieving Redskins." There was bound to be trouble. One young Indian buck came galloping into camp with a frightened white woman named Fanny Kelly bouncing on the horse in front of him.

Sitting Bull and his Strong Hearts took the woman to Fort Sully and returned her to her distracted husband. For this act they received no thanks—not even the feast they expected. At that, they fared better than two other Sioux chiefs who at the same time returned another white captive, Mrs. Eubanks. The Sioux risked their own lives and paid many horses to get Mrs. Eubanks from the Cheyennes in order to return her to Fort Laramie. As a reward for this act they were hanged from the branch of a cottonwood tree.

In the meantime agent Fitzpatrick was busy making preparations for a big meeting of all the Plains tribes for a Treaty Council.

This great meeting took place near Fort Laramie on September 1, 1851. For days the Indians streamed in from all directions, the Sioux, Arapahoes and Cheyennes mingling in greatest friendliness. There was, however, considerable tension among the army officers, for the real test would come when the hereditary enemies of these people, the Snakes and Crows came in. There were two hundred soldiers present. They should be able to control the situation.

When word came that the Shoshones or Snakes, led by Chief Washakie, were approaching a wave of excitement

ran through the waiting tribes. Some trivial act might well
set off a powder keg.

Toward Laramie Peak a long line of dust was observed.
Then the Shoshones came into view like a long snake inch-
ing down the valley. When they came closer it was seen
that the braves in front wore their war regalia. Jim Brider,
a former trapper, now a trader, known throughout the
length and breadth of the land, was with them.

"Boots and Saddles" was sounded and the soldiers leaped
to their horses and the cannons were wheeled to a con-
spicuous position—to be ready for an emergency.

Sitting Bull, on his black war horse, rode to the fore-
ground of his camp and sat with a stolid expression on his
face. The "paper chief," Conquering Bear, rode up and
before the camp, reminding the tribes that they were all
here for a friendly purpose. But no one paid any attention
to him. He wasn't their own leader—merely one named
by the Blue Coat chief. He didn't count.

As the Snakes came closer a few Sioux squaws started
keening for relatives who had died in battle with these
ancient enemies.

As Washakie, with his war bonnet tail fluttering in the
breeze, started the descent of a small hill close to the valley
of the fort a young Sioux leaped on his pony, gave the war
cry and rushed toward the chief, his bow and arrow in
hand. As he was about to let his arrow fly a French interpreter, who happened to be on his horse, galloped toward the Sioux brave and yanked him from his horse.

Pandemonium broke loose, but the soldiers quickly
herded the Snakes to the side of the fort opposite the Sioux
and Sitting Bull sternly commanded his people to be peace-

ful. This might have been one of the bloodiest Indian
battles in history, but the moment of danger passed and
the Treaty Council continued. The night was spent in
feasting and dancing. Then in the morning every Indian
man, woman and child, in his best regalia, came toward the
Council circle, each tribe singing its special song or exe-
cuting its special dance.

The Black Robe, Father De Smet, was there with a delegation of Indians. For the occasion the chiefs had all been
loaned generals' uniforms, with gilt swords to hang at their
sides. They may be forgiven for strutting a bit, in their new
uniforms. The soldiers were hard put to restrain their grins
at the sight of painted faces, long streaming black hair and
moccasined feet in combination with the generals' uniforms.

The chiefs met with the commissioners in the center of
the circle. The calumet was passed and the pipe ceremony
given; then Indian Superintendent Mitchell rose to say that
he and Fitzpatrick had been sent by the Great Father at
Washington to make peace with the tribes. True, the buffalo
were becoming scarce but the Great Father would make
repayment. He wanted the great Medicine Road kept open
and would build military posts along it to supply and protect the emigrants and the Indians. Each nation would have
its own boundaries for hunting and living and all would
be sweetness and light on the prairies.

The "paper chief" then rose and expressed thanks and
agreed to everything Mitchell had said. Then the Indian
chiefs flocked around and touched their hands to the piece
of paper Mitchell handed them. So the Treaty was "signed."
But through it all Sitting Bull sat astride his black horse
like a bronze statue. He did not put his hand to the paper.
The whole performance seemed meaningless to him. All

he asked was for his people to be left alone to live their lives in the good old way. If the Hunkpapas remained un- molested he would do his best to keep his people from molesting the palefaces. The problem was as simple as that to him. He did not want the white man's presents nor his annuities. The Hunkpapas could take care of themselves with the help of their buffalo brothers.

CHAPTER EIGHT

One Chief of All the Sioux

SINCE the establishment of Fort Laramie in 1849, Sitting Bull and his people had frequent dealings with Jim Bordeaux, the trader near there and at other trading posts and these dealings were entirely peaceable. The Hunkpapa chief had no objections to traders, but his uneasiness over the increasing numbers of white-topped wagons was growing. The same uneasiness was spreading through all of the Sioux bands and at Sun Dance time they all gathered near the Standing Rock, the sacred landmark that resembled a woman turned to stone. The purpose of this gathering was to select a chief of their own choosing to act as chief of all the Sioux.

Excitement rippled like wind over prairie grass through the combined Indian villages. Never had there been such an event as this in which a single chief was to be inaugurated to rule over several tribes. The Indian agent tried to bring this about with his "paper chief," but no one outside his own band paid any attention to Conquering Bear.

There had been little dispute among the Sioux bands as to their choice of leader. Sitting Bull's election was practically unanimous.

Four chiefs, Four Horns, Loud-Voiced Hawk, Red Horn and Running Antelope, carried a buffalo robe to the lodge of Sitting Bull. They spread the robe on the ground, led Sitting Bull to it and had him seat himself upon it, then holding it by the four corners, they carried him to the ceremonial lodge.

The pipe was lighted, the mouthpiece was pointed toward the earth that it might make them strong, then to the four winds that no ill winds should blow upon them, then to the sun that it might light their way.

The pipe passed from left to right around the circle, as the sun moves. Every chief inhaled a puff or two, and exhaled with a prayer which the smoke would carry up to the *Wakan Tanka.*

The pipe was a very special one and was a gift to Sitting Bull as his badge of office and remained one of his most treasured belongings the rest of his life.

It was decorated with duck feathers which, being im-
pervious to water and wind, symbolized the same qualities
in the great chief. Because a pipe was used in prayer it was
given to him to use in praying for the people who had
chosen him as leader.

Numerous speeches were made telling of Sitting Bull's
bravery, his generosity, his kindness to animals and people,
his mercy to captives, his brave deeds, his many coups.

Four Horns made the main speech, saying, "Because of
your courage on the battlefield and your reputation as the
bravest warrior in all our bands, we have elected you the
chief of the whole Sioux Nation, our head war chief. It is
your duty to see that the nation is fed, that we have plenty.
When you say 'fight' we shall fight. When you say 'make
peace,' we shall make peace."

Crazy Horse was appointed second in command.

Black Moon, the shaman Sun Dreamer, reminded Sitting
Bull of the two halves of his duty.

"You are first," he said, "to think always of *Wakan
Tanka,* the one above. Second, you are to use all of your
powers to care for your people, and especially the poor."

Sitting Bull solemnly went through the pipe ceremony
to pledge these things. He was then given a splendid bow
with ten arrows and a flint-lock gun.

Running Antelope told him to be like the eagle, strong,
self-reliant, fearless.

Then they brought out the most magnificent war bonnet
Sitting Bull had ever seen. The brow band was beautifully
embroidered with porcupine quills and ermine pendants.
The crown was of shining black and white eagle plumes.
It had a trailing double tail that dragged the ground. Each
feather stood for some brave deed of the warrior who had

donated it. Thus it symbolized the combined valor of the entire Teton Sioux Nation. With this war bonnet he was ceremoniously crowned.

He was then led outside where a fine white horse, gorgeously caparisoned, awaited him. He was lifted into the saddle and all the braves lined up to follow him. Each was garbed in deerskin shirts, decorated with porcupine quills, and fringed with hair. Faces were painted as if for war. Lances were held high in the air and shields were carried uncovered.

Sitting Bull sat his horse with splendid dignity, but out of the corner of his eye he saw the gorgeous procession of prancing horses and colorfully decked warriors as they paraded around the camp circle chanting and his heart swelled with pride. His spirit rose as if on eagle wings bearing a prayer of thanksgiving to the *Wakan Tanka* and a song rose to his lips:

> "Ye tribes, behold me.
> The chiefs of old are gone;
> Myself I shall take courage."

He fully realized the great responsibility that now lay on his shoulders. His heart felt strong for the tasks ahead, but uneasiness lay on his spirit like a dark shadow. His ever-alert intuition told him there was trouble ahead for his people.

Perhaps matters would have remained peaceful for a considerable time longer had it not been for a colossal blunder by the whites. It was in August of 1854. A number of tribes were gathered near Fort Laramie to receive their annuities. Some of Sitting Bull's men had brought furs for trade.

A Mormon caravan was passing the Brûlé camp when one of the emigrants' cows became lame and fell behind.

Several young braves, thinking the cow was deserted, killed it and invited their friends to a feast.

When the Brûlé chief, Bear That Scatters, heard about the incident he went to the fort and reported the affair and offered to pay for the animal. Having been one of the signers of the Treaty, he was eager to live up to its terms to the best of his understanding. Meantime, the Mormon had reported his cow as "stolen."

Things were deadly dull for the fifty soldiers garrisoned in the "Middle of Nowhere." They ached for a little excitement. Lieutenant Fleming decided that the Indians should not be allowed to go unpunished for a single depredation. He sent Lieutenant Grattan to arrest the guilty Indian who, by the way, was a Miniconjou visiting some Brûlé relatives.

Grattan had been bored nearly to insanity. He craved some excitement and the chance to be mentioned in dispatches to Washington. He was to get more than his wish. He was about to make history.

"I hope to God we have a fight," he cried, as, taking an interpreter and twenty-eight soldiers, he rode to the Brûlé camp and demanded that the thief who stole the cow should be given up instantly.

Any Indian considered himself disgraced for life if arrested and confined. Straight Foretop, the Miniconjou, said, "I have a gun with plenty of balls and powder. I have a bow and a quiver full of arrows. If the Blue Coats want me they will have to kill me first."

Grattan now had to use force to capture the Indian or face the humiliation of failing in his mission. He told his men to get the Miniconjou.

Chief Bear came from his tipi. "My friends," he cried. "We do not wish there to be fighting . . ."

He did not finish, for the soldiers shot him as he stood beside his lodge.

In fifteen minutes there was not a soldier of Grattan's command alive.

So happened the first massacre on the Plains. It was a white man's fault.

When Sitting Bull heard of the massacre, he herded his Hunkpapas away to the Black Hills as fast as they could travel so they would not be mixed up in the affair.

Sitting Bull and his people had nothing to do with this matter. It, however, was like the uncorking of the dam of events that was to sweep over all of the Sioux, although Sitting Bull and a handful of his followers were to be the last to be swept to destruction.

Meantime, there was no stemming the onrush of the white settlers. On and on they came in an ever-growing stream. Often Sitting Bull stood on the hilltop shading his eyes as he watched the never-ending caravan. It seemed to him that the land of the rising sun must be emptied of all its inhabitants. Uneasiness was growing in his heart. In a vague way he knew that some day the palefaces would put an end to his good medicine. Somehow, some day they would destroy him. His jaw firmed as he determined to put off that evil day as long as possible.

One day as he stood watching from his hilltop vantage point he heard a clattering of hoofs in the distance. Then the horse appeared, his rider lying low on its neck. He waited to see what was chasing the speeding horseman but nothing appeared. The same thing happened every day. At a different time another rider came from the opposite way. It was very puzzling. Nothing was chasing the riders and they seemed to be pursuing nothing. Sitting Bull shook his head in bewilderment over the incomprehensible doings of the white men.

Later on when he went to Fort Laramie to trade he met one of the riders, a mere boy, who said his name was Bill Cody. He was a "Pony Express rider," he said.

"Why he ride so fast?" Sitting Bull asked his friend, Kit Carson, who was there. Carson spoke the Sioux language and told the chief that Pony Express riders carried mail, those pieces of paper with queer bird-track marks that seemed to have some meaning to white men.

One day in midwinter Sitting Bull had been out hunting and came upon some of his young men grappling with what he first thought was a shaggy bear. When he came closer he saw that his men had captured one of the Express riders in an attempt, no doubt, to see what he carried that made him ride so fast. The rider was putting up a fight and the Sioux were getting rough with him.

Sitting Bull ordered them away and had the young man, who was dressed in a buffalo-robe coat, climb on his horse and took him to camp.

One of the Sioux who had captured the rider was Gall, an ambitious fellow who would have liked to be in Sitting Bull's moccasins. He never missed a chance to challenge Sitting Bull's leadership. Now he insisted that the captive be put to death. Sitting Bull declared that he had adopted the boy as his son. Although the chief now had two wives and several children he had the adoption habit and was forever adding some one else to his brood.

There was quite an argument in camp over the fate of the captive, but finally Sitting Bull won and took to himself a new son.

The lad was Frank Grouard, but Sitting Bull named him Standing Bear because he had looked like one in his big buffalo-robe coat when he first saw him. Later he was called Grabber, the Indian name for bear.

Grabber took to Indian life like a buffalo to his wallow. He lived with the Sioux for six years. Then he finally escaped and joined Connor's troops and repaid Sitting Bull's kindness by scouting against him.

There was no end to the incomprehensible things the palefaces did. Lately they had been putting up branchless dead trees in an endless line across the Plains. Then they tied these poles together with singing wires. In some way, through means of these dead trees and wires, the white men were able to send messages to someone several sleeps away. It was quite amazing. Sitting Bull himself examined several of these branchless trees and even held his ear against them but could hear no talking. Truly the white man's medicine must be good.

Sitting Bull's heart toward the white man was good, at least to the extent of live and let live, until "the year the white man massacred the Indians," 1864.

Over in the valley of Sand Creek in what is now Colorado, another stop was being pulled from the dam that was to loose red destruction upon the Plains.

It was a fanatical person who started it all. Then acting as a Colonel in the 2nd Colorado Volunteer Cavalry, Chivington was sent to bring in some troublesome Cheyennes and Arapahoes. He did not find the hostiles but he did find a camp of Cheyennes under War Bonnet and White Antelope. These natives had been promised protection at this place.

To Chivington all Indians looked alike and "the only good Indian was a dead Indian." He knew that these weren't the hostiles he was after, but that mattered not to him. They were Indians.

Although Black Kettle hoisted the American flag over his tipi to show that he was friendly, Chivington gave the order to fire and dazed men, women and children were mowed down and scalped.

White Antelope was killed before his tipi, but Black Kettle escaped and carried the pipe to all of the Plains tribes. He smoked the pipe with Sitting Bull and told of the outrage upon his village.

After the war-pipe ceremony with Black Kettle, Sitting Bull rose, his dark eyes snapping and his voice vibrating with fury. He cried:

"From this time on my hand is raised against the white man. His heart is black and he speaks with the crooked tongue. He is bent on our destruction. My heart is now bad against the lying paleface."

He sent runners to all of the Sioux tribes telling of his decision and asking the Sioux tribes to unite against the common enemy.

And so the deluge of blood was loosed upon the Plains.

Government officials deplored Chivington's wanton outrage. Their official report said:

"It scarcely has its parallel in the records of Indian brutality. Fleeing women, holding up their hands and praying for mercy, were shot down; infants were killed and scalped in derision; men were tortured and mutilated in a way which would put to shame the savages of interior Africa. No one will be astonished that a war ensued which cost the government $30,000,000 and carried conflagration and death to the border settlements. During the spring and summer of 1865 no less than 8,000 troops were withdrawn from the effective forces engaged against the rebellion to meet this Indian War."

CHAPTER NINE

Sitting Bull Defends His Hunting Grounds

AFTER Sand Creek the sound of the tom-toms echoed over the prairies night after night and by day the smoke signals rose in cloudlike puffs, and mirror signals flashed from hill to hill.

The tension on the Plains was not eased any by the establishment of the Bozeman Trail, a road that cut straight through the Sioux hunting paradise near the Big Horns—

country the white men solemnly promised should be Sioux territory.

Sitting Bull had cautioned his braves to stay away from the whites' great Medicine Road (The Oregon Trail). He had tried to keep them safe in the Big Horn or Black Hills countries, and now here were the whites traveling with their usual clatterdy-bang through this last hunting ground. This time Sitting Bull did not even try to keep his braves from making trouble.

The Indians in what are now Kansas, Nebraska, Colorado and Wyoming, were on the war path. The year of the Red Moon (1865) is called the Bloody Year Upon the Plains. The Sioux came out victorious in a number of skirmishes and with each victory gained firearms and self-confidence.

Sitting Bull's contempt of the white man was increasing. He said that whenever the Indians were in need all they had to do was kill a few white men, then there would be a new treaty of peace (soon to be broken by the white men) and they would be given anything they wanted as peace offerings.

Sitting Bull's young braves discovered the value of the government supply trains loaded with blankets, food, clothing and ammunition and they made special efforts to capture these. Much of the stolen goods was of little use to them. One of their favorite pastimes was to take a bolt of cloth and holding one end, let the other bounce along the prairie until it was unwound and then the Indian would gallop away with the long streamer floating after him. Sometimes the Sioux would capture the payroll for the soldiers but the money meant nothing to them except something to scatter to the wind.

Chivington sowed a breeze for which the white men were

reaping a whirlwind. The government, with a great show of making things right, in 1865 offered the Sioux the Harney-Sanborne Treaty providing for the safe passage of the white men over the Bozeman Trail. Man Afraid Of His Horses and Spotted Tail were induced to sign the Treaty— an act for which they were shunned by their people. Sitting Bull and the brilliant young War Chief, Crazy Horse, refused to sign.

Sitting Bull was not much of an orator, but what he said was listened to with respect. The country through which the Bozeman Trail passed was becoming growingly precious to the Sioux as the buffalo were being wantonly slaughtered by the whites on the Plains. The Big Horn country abounded with flocks of mountain sheep, droves of elk and deer, as well as buffalo.

"The *Wakan Tanka* made this country for us, his red children," Sitting Bull said. "Unless we wish to starve we must keep the lying white man from this, our last hunting ground."

The government sent the Powder River Expedition under General Connor to bring the troublesome Sioux "under control." Although the treacherous Grabber, whose life Sitting Bull saved and whom he treated like a brother, was acting as Connor's scout, Sitting Bull and Crazy Horse made monkeys of the troops by leading them a merry chase over the worst sort of country where the soldiers could not obtain food or water.

Sitting Bull's contempt for the white man was growing. A sense of humor was always strong in him and came to the surface once in a trader's post when he felt he was being cheated by the trader. When the latter became disagreeable about the matter Sitting Bull leaped over the counter and took charge and to the great delight of his warriors, mimicked the trader. He handed down bolts of cloth, ammunition and all kinds of goods. But before making a trade he examined each robe and pelt, finding fault with it, no matter how fine it was and claiming that his goods were so superior he would not consider a trade without putting the valuation of the furs way down. His impersonation of the trader was so clever and true that the natives were doubled up with laughter. In the end, though, they got full value for their pelts.

The government sent a new commission to deal with the Sioux. The white men were already swarming over the Bozeman Trail on the way to the gold fields in Montana, but the Indians continuously made trouble for them. Danger, however, never deterred white men when they were after gold.

Then the government sent yet another commission to Fort Laramie to deal with the problem. They sent for all the Sioux chiefs and tendered Sitting Bull, chief of all the Sioux, chosen by the red men themselves, a special invitation. The commission had found out by this time that the Indians paid no attention to the chief they selected.

The object of the commission was not only to obtain the Sioux' permission for the white men to use the Bozeman Trail unmolested, but also to obtain permission to erect forts along this famous trail.

The white men spoke long and persuasively and many were the gifts that were passed out. A few of the sub-chiefs, the "woman-hearted" ones like Man Afraid Of His Horses and Spotted Tail and especially Gall, who fancied himself as an orator, spoke in favor of signing the Treaty.

Everyone looked to Sitting Bull, chief of all the Sioux.

His medicine was great. His people would follow his lead—
all except Gall who was jealous of Sitting Bull's power and
always pulled in the opposite direction. But through the
meeting the great chief and Medicine Man sat silent, with
a bored and disgusted expression on his broad face. He
had not spoken but it was plain to see he was not in favor
of the forts. Finally he rose to speak.

"Behold, my friends, the spring is come; the earth has
gladly received the embraces of the sun, and we shall soon
see the results of their love! Every seed is awakened, and all
animal life. It is through this mysterious power that we,
too, have our being, and we therefore yield to our neighbors, even to our animal neighbors, the same right as ourselves to inhabit this vast land.

"Yet hear me, friends! We have now to deal with another
people, small and feeble when our forefathers first met
with them, but now great and overbearing. Strangely
enough, they have a mind to till the soil, and the love of
possessions is a disease in them. These people have made
many rules that the rich may break, but the poor may not!
They have a religion in which the poor worship, but the
rich will not. They even take tithes of the poor and weak
to support the rich and those who rule. They claim this
mother of ours, the earth, for their own use and fence their
neighbors away from her, and deface her with their buildings and their refuse. They compel her to produce out of
season, and when sterile she is made to take medicine in
order to produce again. All this is sacrilege.

"This nation is like a spring freshet, it overruns its
banks and destroys all who are in its path. We cannot dwell
side by side. Only seven years ago we made a treaty by
which we were assured that the buffalo country should be

left to us forever. Now they threaten to take that from us also. My brothers, shall we submit? Or shall we say to them, 'First kill me before you can take the land of my fathers.' "

There was a humming sound as of many bees when Sitting Bull sat down. The Indian agent leaped to his feet and recommenced his persuasive arguments. The other white men did likewise.

In the midst of the council while one of the commissioners was making a speech telling of how good the white man's heart was toward his red brothers, Sitting Bull leaped to his feet and pointed to a cloud of dust in the distance.

Ordinarily the chief was a commonplace-looking man with a plain, expressionless face, but oftentimes when he spoke an inner force shone through that made him the most dynamic of men. It was at such times the Hunkpapas knew the *Wakan Tanka* was speaking to them through their leader.

"From the land of the rising sun the white grandfather is sending his Blue Coats," Sitting Bull cried. "Even while the lying words come from the crooked tongues of the black-hearted palefaces, soldiers come to build their forts—to take away our last hunting ground—the land they promised us for our own. Will we starve to death like dogs or fight like men? Sitting Bull will fight the crooked-tongued white man until he dies. Those of you who are men, follow me. The women stay behind."

He stalked from the council room and all the Sioux followed him—none of them was woman-hearted today.

The blue column Sitting Bull had seen approaching was the troops under General Henry B. Carrington on their way to the Powder River Country to erect a row of forts. Even while the white men were pretending to negotiate for

the Powder River Country, they were making ready to
take it by conquest. And that they considered the conquest
would be an easy one was shown by the fact that a number
of the soldiers and officers took their wives and families
along.

They had not reckoned with the power of Sitting Bull
to unite all the Sioux Nations and gather to them the Crows,
Cheyennes and Arapahoes—ancient enemies now willing
to join forces against the common foe. Nor had they reckoned with a brilliant young war chief of the Sioux, Crazy
Horse. He it was who had led the force that wiped out
Grattan's command. Sitting Bull recently appointed him
main war chief. Events on the Plains were rapidly rising to
a crescendo—a terrible and bloody climax.

CHAPTER TEN

The Bloody Year on the Plains

WHERE once had been only the sounds of running water, of wind in the trees, of song of birds, now rang other, more discordant noises: the sound of hammers, of ax, the buzzing of a sawmill.

It was in the Moon of The Cherries Turn Red that the Blue Coat chief commenced to build Fort Phil Kearny, soon to be called Fort Perilous. Two days later Sitting Bull's men attacked the wood train, taking two scalps and sending three other men hurrying with bleeding wounds to the fort.

Constantly the supply trains and wood trains were attacked. Sitting Bull vowed that the white men at the fort should know no peace. The nearest forest from which lumber for the buildings could be obtained was seven miles away from the fort. The wood trains were continuously attacked and hectored, but still the building went on. Once the fort was finished and reinforced the Blue Coats would be in a good position to drive the Sioux from their hunting ground.

As was his frequent habit, Sitting Bull fasted, took the sweat bath and went off into the hills alone. He stood facing the sun and put himself in communion with the Great Mystery until the Vision came. In it he saw his outstretched hands filled with blue-coated soldiers. The Vision was very real—one of the most real he ever had. He went down among his people well content that his medicine was good.

He called a big council of all the tribes and told them of his Vision. They would, he told them, remain in the hills during the winter, although this was not their custom. Their meat was made; their tipis were snug; they would remain in the shadow of the Big Horns and drive the Blue Coats from their country.

Messengers came from Fort Laramie to tell Sitting Bull that the agent wished all of the Sioux to come in; that they would be given much food and many presents. The season of the big snow and the popping wood was soon to come. The Sioux would be comfortable at the agency.

"Phaugh!" Sitting Bull spat out the word. He had nothing but contempt for the loafer Indians who hung around Fort Laramie, living on the white man's rations.

He looked around the council circle at the dark faces thrown into weird shadows by the fire. The faces were sullen, unyielding, and the eyes glinted fiercely. He saw that his power over these men held.

"The white men speak only with crooked tongues," he cried. "Let them keep their presents. We will keep our land."

The Brûlé messengers went on to explain that the Blue Coats would chase them away. They had many wagon guns coming. Many more Blue Coats. There was a new chief among them who called himself Fetterman. He said that with eighty Blue Coats he would wipe out the Sioux Nation.

"Phaugh!" Sitting Bull snarled. Then he made the angry snorting noise a wild animal emits before it charges—the sound Indian warriors always make before going into battle.

"Tell the Blue Coat chief, Fetterman, that we will be ready," was the message Sitting Bull sent back to Fort Laramie by the Brûlé loafer.

The Indian camp along the Tongue River numbered one thousand tipis. Never had so many tribes gathered in one place.

Sitting Bull knew that more soldiers had got through in the night to the hated fort on the Piney. He laid his plans and bided his time, but it was hard to restrain the impetuosity of his young men, who attacked the wood train time and again or who scalped the stock herders, and were now eager to count coups.

Sitting Bull knew that this was not the time for mere counting of coups. Warfare for the Sioux had come to have a grimmer meaning than the gathering of individual honors to boast about around the campfire. Now they were fighting for their very existence. They must either drive the soldiers from their hunting grounds or perish themselves. They must make plans, as the Blue Coats did, and fight in a body, as they did, rather than each warrior for himself. It would be difficult to make the young braves, greedy for coups, learn to fight this way.

He gathered his fighters together and talked to them and his medicine was good that day. They listened to him and agreed. He told them that the white men had many guns and much powder and balls; the Sioux had few weapons besides their bows and arrows. They must make a trap for the Blue Coats, get them bunched together like buffaloes and then make a surround.

"We have tried this before," Sitting Bull said, "but always the plan failed because some young warrior, thinking only of himself, was off to count first coup. This time we must not fail or we will die. We must have a handful of brave warriors who will act as decoys to bring the Blue Coats into our trap. But these decoys must not strike. They must act afraid—run from the soldiers. Then when we have them in our trap by the big rocks we who have been hiding behind the hill will make the surround and kill them like buffaloes."

"Hau! Hau!" the braves cried in agreement. They knew that their chief's medicine was good. They would trap the young Blue Coat chief Fetterman and his men. The Sioux did not care for this method of fighting. It did not accord with their motions of bravery. But Sitting Bull was right. They must now fight the white man in his own way or die.

Hump was chosen to act as leader for the decoys. Crazy

Horse was to lead the attack when the soldiers were bunched in the trap in the rough country. Sitting Bull was to go to a hilltop to watch with his farseeing glasses the actions of the wood train and the troop and to make medicine.

It was the Moon When The Trees Crack With Frost (January). The weather was stinging cold.

As they waited the impatient soldiers made the snorting noise of the angry grizzly.

At daybreak a handful of brave warriors galloped out with raised war shields to attack the wood train.

Bang! Bang! Bang! The rapid pop of the signal shots signifying trouble to the wood train rang out over the crisp air.

Sitting Bull stood on the hilltop watching through his farseeing glasses. He saw the soldiers stream through the gate of the fort, and gallop toward the wood train. Then, at the right moment, he flapped his blanket in the air— the signal for Hump and his decoys to come to lure the soldiers into the rough country. They had left their horses back in the valley, for the soldiers followed Indians afoot more readily.

The Blue Coats seemed to be stepping into the trap— both the horse soldiers and the walking soldiers. But they paused atop the Lodge Trail Ridge and Sitting Bull held his breath. Would they turn back, or continue on into the valley? The Blue Coats were not fools, he knew. Yet, if this young Blue Coat chief, Fetterman, was so eager to wipe out the Sioux Nation he might be reckless enough to go on.

Through his own glasses Sitting Bull saw the soldier leader search the landscape with his far-looking glasses. Hump and his men were playing their parts well, acting afraid of the soldiers and anxious to get away. The other warriors were laying low—not being too ready this time to count coup and scare the soldiers away.

At last the Blue Coats' horsemen came riding down into the valley, the walking soldiers stepping smartly after them. They had no wagon gun.

When the soldiers were down in the valley at the forks of the Peno by the big rocks, Sitting Bull gave the signal and the Indians led by Crazy Horse, Lone Bear, Big Nose, He Dog and others came charging from behind the hill giving their terrifying war whoops.

The soldiers fought bravely, bunching, as the Indians wanted them to do, and trying to fight their way up the steep icy slope, but Crazy Horse's men cut off their retreat. In an unbelievably short time it was all over. There was not a Blue Coat left alive of the eighty with whom Fetterman planned to ride through the Sioux Nation.

It was bitter cold. Some of the Indians were wounded and the blood froze as it oozed from the bullet holes.

Quickly the Indians took the scalps and yanked the uniforms from the soldiers' bodies. They set up howls of delight at the fine new guns and the ammunition obtained from this fight.

Before long a new group of soldiers with wagon guns appeared on Lodge Trail Ridge. The Indians had had enough fighting for one day and retreated to gloat over their triumph beside their snug tipi fires.

They did not know that they had wiped out over half of Carrington's command and that if they had attacked the fort that night they could have taken it.

A severe blizzard came up and they were content to hug their cozy tipi fires while a rider was sent from the fort through the storm to Fort Laramie for reinforcements.

CHAPTER ELEVEN

The Wagon Box Fight

THE year the Blue Coats were slain (1866) was the coldest the old men had ever known. The elk, the deer, the buffaloes had gone. Even the wolves deserted the country, following the scattered herds, no doubt. The meat parfleches were flat. The hunters were hard put to supply food for the great camp on the Tongue River.

The soldiers and the woodmen remained within the fort and Sitting Bull's warriors hugged their campfires and enjoyed the thick winter smell of the tipi and its comfortable warmth. They holed up like grizzly bears and waited for the Moon of Green Grass.

It seemed as if the Moons of Popping Trees and Sore

Eyes would never end. Then all of a sudden the sun was warm, green grass thrust tender points through the soft earth. Birds were busy and streams were laughing. Then the red blood began to race in the veins of the warriors again and Sitting Bull strode up and down in front of his lodge, his brain busy with plans for destroying the hated fort on the Piney.

His young men under Crazy Horse, however, were too impatient to wait for plans. They wanted coups. Incessantly they hectored the wood train, the herders, the supply trains.

It was during the Moon When The Chokecherries Are Red that the thing happened that made many of his people doubt the continuing strength of Sitting Bull's medicine.

The wood train went out to the forest of the Big Horns. Crazy Horse's warriors were to attack. Sitting Bull himself agreed to the plans. He hadn't gone to the hills for his Vision Quest but since Fetterman's Blue Coats had been wiped out he had no reason to believe that his power might be waning.

The wood train went out as usual. The woodcutters put up their little tents at the edge of the woods and the Blue Coats stayed to guard them. But they did a strange thing this time. They took their wagon boxes, fourteen of them, off the wheels and made them into a hollow square, like a fort or corral. Within this enclosure the soldiers picketed their horses and stayed in there themselves during the night, leaving two watchers to walk around the square.

At daybreak the Sioux were up daubing war paint on themselves and their ponies. Sitting Bull tried to talk to them, to get them to make some plan to fight together, but they were in no mood to listen to advice. Their blood was hot for glory and for coups. They were eager to fight in the old Indian way.

Crazy Horse led a handful of decoys out to draw the soldiers' fire. As soon as one of the guards fired the Hunkpapas came from behind the hills, galloping pell-mell, giving the war whoop. There was no stopping them. It was each man for himself.

The decoys made short work of the guards.

On, on, the whooping, galloping warriors came, their arrows going plop, plop, into the wooden wagons and then they were stopped. There was no standing against that solid blast of fire that came from the wagon boxes. The Indians had never faced anything like it. They raced for the shelter of the hills.

Crazy Horse told his men to dismount and make the foot charge. This they did, more cautiously. First they ran fast, war shields raised, bows ready. Then swiftly they would loose arrow or lance and drop into a buffalo wallow or other low place. They got quite close to the wagon corral in this manner before the blast of fire mowed them down.

Again they retreated to talk things over. They could not understand how the soldiers could fire so fast. It seemed they did not need to stop to reload their guns.

Sitting Bull's eyes were blazing. He strode up and down telling his men to be careful. Too many warriors were getting killed. But the Dakotas charged, only to meet that withering blast once more. They retreated again behind the hills to lick their wounds. This time they did not attack. Instead they took the two guns obtained from the slain pickets and examined them. Then the secret of the Blue Coats' unceasing fire was discovered. They now had fire-again (repeating) guns.

The Sioux had never seen their chief so worked-up as he was that day striding up and down, haranguing his warriors.

"We must have guns!" he cried. "Guns and guns and more guns. Go to the agencies. Crawl. Beg. Steal. Use any trick to get guns. We can no longer fight the white man with bows and arrows and war clubs. Even though we have the strong heart of the grizzly, it is not enough without guns. Get guns, my braves, and we will face the Blue Coats and take their hair!"

After the wagon-box defeat a number of his warriors deserted Sitting Bull. Yet he managed to hold a goodly number of them together—enough to make life a long drawn-out nightmare for those at Fort Phil Kearny.

His warriors made so much trouble that another Commission was sent to Fort Laramie to try to get all the chiefs to sign the new peace paper.

Loafer messengers were sent to try to persuade Sitting Bull to come to the big council. They rode fine ponies given them by the agent. They had fine new leather saddles and new blankets and white man's clothes. They brought promises of many fine presents to any of the Sioux who would go in. But Sitting Bull's people were well fed. They wanted none of the white man's presents.

All they wanted, Sitting Bull told the messengers, was to be left alone on the hunting grounds promised to the Sioux. His hand was raised against the white man and his heart was bad toward him because of the broken promises. His hand would be raised against the iron trail, too. He refused to go to Fort Laramie.

At length the only white man who had courage to brave the hostile red man in his lair was sent to try to bring

Sitting Bull to terms. It was Father De Smet, the Catholic priest the Indians called the Black Robe.

When runners appeared at the Sioux village on the Powder River, telling of the approach of the Black Robe with his interpreter, Sitting Bull was annoyed. He did not want to be bothered. However, the Black Robe had the reputation, throughout the length and breadth of the lands, of speaking with the straight tongue. His heart was good toward the Indians and they knew it, so Sitting Bull agreed to meet with De Smet and hear what he had to say. Yet he was not willing to accept the fact that the Black Robe was a representative of the Great Mystery without the priest's proving his power.

"See that buffalo bull grazing on the plains," the chief said. "If you can go and place your hand on its head I will believe you speak for the Great Spirit. If the bull kills you, I shall know your heart is black like that of other palefaces."

Father De Smet knew that if he were to win the confidence of the chief he must accept this challenge. The great beast did not notice the priest's approach until they were only a few feet apart, then it raised its head and snorted fiercely. Quietly and calmly the priest continued to walk toward the animal and placed his hand on its head. Then he walked back to the camp.

Now Sitting Bull could not refuse to listen respectfully to the brave priest's message. De Smet said, "The Great White Father in Washington wants you to live among your people on your own lands. He will give you plenty of food and warm clothing. You will not be prisoners; you will have your liberty."

Sitting Bull replied, "Black Robe, I hardly sustain myself

beneath the weight of white man's blood I have shed. The whites provoked the war. Their injustices, their indignities to our families, the cruel, unheard of and wholly unprovoked massacre at Fort Lyon (the Chivington Massacre) of hundreds of Cheyenne women and children and old men, shook all the veins which bind and support me. I rose, tomahawk in hand, and I have done all the hurt to the whites that I could. Today you are here and my arms stretch to the ground as if dead. I will listen to your good words. And bad as I have been to the white men, just so good am I ready to become toward them."

Long into the night the two men sat talking earnestly. Sitting Bull declared that he had become the mortal enemy of the whites and fought them with every means in his power because he felt that he was fighting for the existence of his people.

Again he stressed that he wanted only to be left alone. That all he asked was the right for his people to the Big Horns and Black Hills country—merely that the white men live up to the terms of their own treaties.

The next day the council for all the tribes was held. Father De Smet later described this most unique of all meetings in his *Letters of Travel*. All the natives were dressed in their most splendid regalia for the occasion. The chiefs and head men sat with the priest on robes in the center of a huge circle of Sioux. The pipe was first offered to Father De Smet, then passed solemnly around the circle, its blue smoke twisting upward carrying the prayer to the *Wakan Tanka*.

Father De Smet then rose and spoke to them in simple language, through an interpreter, beseeching them to accept the offering of peace he was bringing them from the Great White Father.

Black Moon, as official orator of the Sioux, made reply.

He rose, calumet in hand, and addressing his people, said: "Lend an ear to my words." Then he raised the calumet solemnly to heaven and lowered it to earth; thus invoking heaven and earth as his witnesses. Then he said: "The Black Robe has made a long journey to come among us; his presence makes my heart glad, and with all my heart I wish him welcome to my country. His words are good and filled with truth.

"Still, our hearts are sore; they have received deep wounds. These wounds remain to be healed. A cruel war has desolated and impoverished our country; the torch of war was not kindled by us; it was the Sioux and Cheyennes east and south of us who raised the war first, to revenge themselves for the white man's cruelties and injustice. We were forced to take part.

"Today when we ride over our Plains we find them spotted with blood; not the blood stains of buffalo and deer killed in the chase, but those of our own comrades. The game have quitted our immense Plains. May it not be the odor of human blood that puts them to flight? The white men cut up our country with roads. They build forts on our hunting grounds and mount thunders on them. They are ruining our land. The soil is ours. Here our fathers were born and are buried. We have been forced to hate the whites. Let them treat us like brothers and the war will cease. Let them stay at home; we will never go to trouble them. Let us throw a veil over the past; let it be forgotten."

Sitting Bull then rose and after the pipe ceremony said:

"What Black Moon said finds echo in my heart. We do not want the white man's annuities. We do not want trouble. We want our land so we can hunt and live. We welcome the traders but we do not want our land filled up with white men. Yet my people will go with you to talk with the Great Father's white chiefs at Fort Rice. We would like to live at peace with the palefaces."

At the end of the meeting there was, as Father De Smet wrote, "Singing that roused the echoes of the hills and a dance that made the ground tremble."

He gave the Indians his banner bearing the name of Jesus and the figure of the Virgin Mary, and to Sitting Bull he gave a large crucifix on a chain that was to be the chief's prized possession all his life.

Father De Smet returned to headquarters and skillfully summarized Sitting Bull's demands. They were, briefly:

"The roads through the Indian hunting grounds must be closed."

"The forts must be abandoned."

"No whites except the traders should be allowed within the Indians' territory."

Only on these terms would Sitting Bull allow the white man's iron horse to go through the country to the south. Reasonable enough demands they were in all conscience. They had first been promised by the white man himself. Sitting Bull did not, himself, go to the meeting at Fort Rice. He said that he had already spoken; there was no need for more words. He sent as his spokesmen, Gall, who he said was as much agency Indian as warrior, and Bull Owl and Running Antelope.

Father De Smet was instrumental in putting across the idea that Sitting Bull meant exactly what he said. His men could put hand to the peace paper on his terms and his terms only.

At length the weary commissioners gave in and made the Treaty of 1868 according to Sitting Bull's own terms. The famous treaty stated: "The United States hereby agrees and stipulates that the country north of the North Platte River and east of the summit of the Big Horn Mountains shall be held and considered to be unceded Indian territory and also stipulates and agrees that no white person or persons shall be permitted to settle upon or occupy any portion of the same; or without consent of the Indians . . . to pass through the same. It is further agreed by the United States that within ninety days after the conclusion of peace with all the bands of the Sioux Nation, the military posts now established in the territory of this article named shall be abandoned and that roads leading to them and by them to the Territory of Montana shall be closed."

Article II provided: ". . . the Sioux had the right to hunt on any lands north of the North Platte River so long as buffalo may range thereon in such numbers as to justify the chase."

The treaty further provided that in the future no treaty would be valid unless it had been signed by three-fourths of the adult males of the tribes.

In the Moon When the Plums Are Ripe the Stars and Stripes was hauled down from above Fort Phil Kearny and the Blue Coats marched out. They weren't out of sight before Sitting Bull's men swarmed in and put the torch to the palisades which had been erected at the cost of so much bloodshed.

For the first time in history American troops had suffered a defeat at the hands of the redskins.

CHAPTER TWELVE

Good Medicine

FOR a time following the visit of the Black Robe and the signing of the treaty life among the Hunkpapas went on much as it had in the good days before the coming of the white man. Again there were hunts and feasts and dancing and visiting back and forth between the bands of Sioux. Now that they no longer needed to stay in a body to fight the Blue Coats, the tribes separated, for hunting and living was easier in smaller groups.

Again the women tanned the buffalo skins and decorated moccasins and wearing apparel beautifully with dyed porcupine quills. Some of the lazier of them preferred to use beads obtained from the white men, but since Sitting Bull frowned on much trading with the whites except for guns and ammunition most of the Hunkpapa women still used quill embroidery.

Now the warriors again worked at making war shields or other war equipment, for the women were not allowed to touch such articles.

Sitting Bull's first wife died and he married the sisters of Gray Eagle. It was a common practice among the Sioux for the men to marry sisters, for usually they got along well together. Since the high death rate among Indian warriors left a surplus of women, it was the custom for each man to take two wives or more.

Sitting Bull's lodge was always swarming with young ones. There were his own children, Her Many Horses, Little Soldier, Standing Holy, Crowfoot and Patala. Then there was his sister Pretty Feather's deaf-and-dumb son John Sitting Bull, whom he had adopted, as well as several other adopted children.

His manner about his own village was always kind, genial and courteous in marked contrast to what it was in the company of white people. Then he was arrogant and insolent, taking no trouble whatever to show his lack of respect for them.

Now he was working on an interesting project—something none of his kinsfolk had ever done. He was writing his autobiography, Indian-fashion, by means of pictographs.

Of course it was common practice for warriors to draw pictures of some of their exploits on their tipis, or on hides to place against the inner tipi walls, but Sitting Bull was drawing all his coups in a book—a blank roll-book of the Thirty-first Regiment of Infantry, obtained from a trader.

Each pictograph contains his own trade-mark—a sitting bull in the upper right-hand corner. He had finished forty of the pictures when the book was stolen by a Yankton Sioux and sold to an army officer at Fort Buford. The original of this unique autobiography is now with the Bureau of American Ethnology in Washington. It consists of forty pictures and carries Bull's history only to 1870, when it was stolen.

The chief, however, did not spend all his time sitting around drawing his autobiography. Indeed, he still had his hands full protecting the hunting grounds of his people, for now the Iron Trail was stretching its iron feelers across the Plains and over it tore the screeching Iron Horse to frighten the game.

The white man's locomotive was a fearsome thing to the Indians—some of them called it the "Fire Boat Walks On Mountains." They believed it carried the Thunder Bird, for they heard its war whoop as it sped along and certainly it could fly from mountain to mountain for they saw it cross a deep ravine without falling. The fact that the locomotive had "flown" across by means of a bridge spanning the ravine did not seem to impress them.

With the coming of the iron trail through the plains country, the white buffalo hunters came to kill the animals for food for the crews building the railroad. One of these men who had once been a Pony Express rider through the Sioux country became a hunter and earned for himself the title "Buffalo Bill." Sitting Bull had heard of him. This man Cody had killed more than four thousand buffaloes, and he was only one man.

Following the hunters who killed for food were the fools who came in on the Iron Horse and killed merely for the fun of it. Then there were the hide hunters who slaughtered the buffaloes merely for the hides and left the huge carcasses to rot on the Plains. Thousands of animals were slaughtered in this way. Stories of this wanton killing were brought to Sitting Bull's ears. A chill of apprehension ran up his spine. Was there never to be an end to the depredations of the white men? He could not imagine life without the buffalo. His people were not suffering yet. There was still good hunting in the Big Horns and the Black Hills. There was not, however, enough hunting for all the hungry tribes that came crowding in as food became scarcer and scarcer in other parts. So the old warfare continued to drive the other tribes from their land.

But *Hopo! Hopo!* Get Going! That was the way the Sioux liked it. It was Indian nature to go to war and gather glory for themselves.

The Crows, as usual, were the most troublesome of the enemy tribes who would hunt on Sitting Bull's own hunting grounds. There was the time during the Hungry Winter when Sitting Bull was out with a hunting party and ran across the trail of thirty-one raiding Crows, north of the mouth of the Powder River. It did not take the Sioux long to get ready for action. They hurried to the village for war paraphernalia and fresh horses and when they learned that the Crows had killed two young Sioux hunters, they gave the war grunt and urged their ponies over the trail of the Crows.

The enemy heard them coming and entrenched themselves in a strategic place in the Bad Lands on a sheer eminence, surrounded by rocky cliffs in the midst of which was a little hollow. It was the perfect spot to stand off a siege, and stand it off they did for two days and two nights.

Sitting Bull was in despair. He could not tell his warriors

to retreat. He would be laughed to shame. He could never again hold up his head before his people. He had with him a hundred braves. They were being held off by thirty-one Crows. He had never been so humiliated in his life.

"Hopo! Hopo! Follow Me," he cried. "I shall climb the cliff. Jump in among them. You follow as quickly as possible."

Not waiting to see whether or not his warriors would agree to such a rash act, he ran out far ahead and scaled the cliff and began cracking skulls right and left with his war club. By the time the other Hunkpapas were atop the eminence, he had several Crows laid out. It was a hand-to-hand fight then, for some of the Sioux could not or would not scale the embankment. Only two Hunkpapas were killed in that battle. That night there was one of the biggest victory dances the Hunkpapas had held for a long time.

Sitting Bull was so busy running off the Crows and other tribes that came to encroach on his hunting grounds that he almost forgot the pesky white men. Word was brought to him that Red Cloud, Man Afraid Of His Horses and Lean Elk were going over the Medicine Road to visit the Great Father in Washington. Sitting Bull was invited to go, too.

"I am busy," he said. "I have no time to go visiting with the White Father."

Another man named Sitting Bull, an Ogalala Sioux, went along, but the chief and Medicine Man stayed in the Big Horns with his own people.

Sitting Bull, however, was not to be allowed to forget the whites for very long. It was the middle of the Moon of Ripe Plums when Gall and some of his warriors came galloping pell-mell into camp, panting that many horse soldiers followed by many walking soldiers were coming up the Yellowstone.

"We will go to meet them," Sitting Bull said calmly. "We will tell them not to come upon our land."

The warriors hurried to get into war clothes and paint. It was thus they always went to meet friends or strangers. And as usual, they carried shields, and war equipment— just in case. . . .

Night was dissolving into day when the Sioux came to the soldier camp in the Yellowstone Valley.

Instantly the Blue Coats came swarming from their tents, firing at the Indians.

It was the usual kind of fighting, with the soldiers crowded behind an embankment, firing incessantly, and the young Indians dashing up to show their bravery. Plenty Rice was killed first. The soldiers tossed his body into the fire. This act threw the young men into a rage. Crazy Horse had never been so daring—he galloped up and down, up and down in front of the soldiers' line.

The old men in the rear kept exclaiming over his bravery, of how good his medicine was. None of the soldiers' bullets could hit him.

Sitting Bull was getting enough of such goings on. So the old ones thought that Crazy Horse was brave, did they? That his medicine was good? Well he would show them who was brave! Whose medicine was good.

He dropped his gun and bow on the ground, drew out his pipe, walked close to the enemy line, sat down cross-legged on the bare ground and calmly puffed his pipe.

For a long moment there was no more firing from behind the embankment. Probably the soldiers were too astonished to fire. Then the bullets began to plop around the chief

like hail, but he calmly sat there. And not a bullet hit him.
When he finished his pipeful, he got up and strolled back
to his horse. The fighting was over and the Sioux loudly
proclaimed that Sitting Bull's act was the bravest they had
ever seen. His medicine was so good it kept away the soldiers' bullets. His power over his people was strengthened
even more.

CHAPTER THIRTEEN

War Clouds Gather

THERE was a peaceful lull on the Plains during 1873-74. The Indians everywhere were keeping their part of the agreement with the government. Sitting Bull was doing his best to keep his young men from making trouble. There was still horse stealing and raiding parties between enemy tribes and the hunting in the Big Horns and the Black Hills was still good. These things were enough to keep any Indian happy.

Although the Sioux loved the Big Horns country because

it was a hunters' paradise, they had especial affection for the Black Hills, for it was sacred ground to them. It was the place where they believed the first man was created. The place held a holy significance to them and they returned here annually to renew their spiritual sources. This was not the only reason, for the place was a veritable heaven on earth. The game was plentiful. The springs were crystal clear and pure. The quiet hills rose in a wooded, protective circle. The great *Wakan Tanka* seemed very near in this pleasant place and the Sioux always looked forward to the time spent in their beloved Black Hills.

By the summer of 1875 Sitting Bull abandoned any idea that the white men would ever leave his people in peace, for Long Hair (Custer) came riding with his troops through the Sioux' sacred Black Hills country. The Indians knew Long Hair well. They had respect for his bravery. They said that he fought somewhat like the Indian, too; that is, he seemed to fight for glory and personal distinction.

Word spread through the tribes then that General Sheridan had sent Long Hair to pick out a location for a military post in the Black Hills. Nevertheless, Sitting Bull prevented his young warriors from molesting the Blue Coats.

The Sioux chief was uneasy—and with very good reason. He did not know it, but when Custer had returned to his post, he had given out a report that there was much gold in the Black Hills. He himself had picked it out from the grass roots.

There was no stopping the rush of gold-seekers to the Black Hills then. The Army sent Custer and his troops to make a pretense of driving the miners out. As the troops marched out of one end of Deadwood, the miners flocked back in at the other end, and there they stayed. Still Sitting Bull managed to keep his warriors in check. He was giving the Great Father a fair chance to live up to his bargain. He took his own tribe far to the north, out of temptation's way. There was frequent trouble between the miners and other Sioux tribes, but Sitting Bull's men were not involved.

A commission was sent asking the Sioux to sell the sacred land of the Black Hills.

Sitting Bull replied: "I have no land to sell. The Black Hills belongs to me. The Great Father said so. We want no white men here. We want the white men to let us alone. If they try to take the Black Hills from us we will fight. This is holy land."

But the miners stayed on the holy land of the Sioux, grubbing away for the yellow dirt that to them meant more than life, safety or honor.

Since the Sioux would not sell the land the miners wanted, the government took steps to get all the Sioux, hostile or otherwise, onto the reservations. Accordingly, late in the Moon of The Middle of Winter (December), in the year of the Terrible Cold, 1875, runners came to the Hunkpapa camp at the mouth of the Powder River bearing word that all Indians must be on their reservations before the 31st of January or "they shall be deemed hostile and treated accordingly by the military force."

The old men of the Sioux tribes say that that winter was the coldest within their memories. The snow lay in deep drifts. Sitting Bull's camp was about two hundred and fifty miles from the Standing Rock agency. Many of his men were scattered on hunting trips. It was absolutely impossible to move women and children over that winter-locked country by the dead line, let alone round up his scattered tribesmen. Even the runners, unhampered as they were, did not get back to the agency within the time set.

Not that Sitting Bull had any intention of trying the impossible. He sent a message back to Sheridan inviting him to come on. The message ended with these words:

"You won't need to bring any guides. You can find me easily. I won't run away."

On receipt of this message the War Department declared Sitting Bull to be hostile and plans were made to deal with him.

Game was scarce that hard winter of '75. The hunters had to work hard to keep the camp supplied, yet Sitting Bull's people fared far better than those on the reservations. A number of agency Indians were deserting and joining the village on the Powder River and they were lean-bellied indeed. They told of the starvation rations—the tough, stringy beef—when they got it at all; the rancid, mouldy bacon, the wormy flour. They told of receiving only one thin blanket for every three people—of the cold, the hunger, the boredom. They were not allowed to have their ceremonial dances, nor to make shields or bows or arrows or do any of the things that would remind them that they were Indians. They must become like white people as quickly as possible. The stories the agency deserters told did not inspire Sitting Bull's people to hurry to the reservation.

While they remained in their snug tipis, sniffing the savory smells that came from the stew kettle, working on war shields, or fashioning bows and talking of coups, plans were being laid far away for the war to be waged on the "hostile" Sioux. Three expeditions were to strike, early in the year while the Indians' ponies would be weak from living on cottonwood bark and while the drifts made it difficult for them to travel. "Three Stars" General Crook was to move northward from Fort Fetterman. General Gibbon was to march eastward from Fort Ellis, and "Long Hair" Custer was to drive westward from Fort Lincoln. As it happened, it was too cold and the snow too deep for the expeditions from the Missouri to the Powder River, so it was decided that Crook would attack from the south.

"Grabber," Frank Grouard, whose life Sitting Bull had saved and who had been befriended and treated like a brother by both Crazy Horse and Sitting Bull, was scouting for Crook. He knew the country and the habits of the Sioux well and led the troops straight to the sleeping camp of Crazy Horse. At first the Indians yielded to panic, as they always did in a surprise attack, but Crazy Horse soon got them under control and shortly had Reynolds' battalion reeling backward. Crook came up to save the command from probable annihilation. Nevertheless, it was a humiliating defeat for Crook's men.

The soldiers had destroyed the supplies of Crazy Horse's village and the hungry, half-frozen Ogalalas sought out Sitting Bull's camp where they were lodged and fed.

Sitting Bull listened in silence to Crazy Horse's story of the unprovoked attack on his sleeping village. Ever since he had smoked the pipe with the Black Robe in the summer of the signing of the peace paper he had made his young warriors keep the peace. He had kept his promises. Even when the hairy-faced diggers in the dirt invaded the sacred Black Hills; even when Long Hair clattered through their sacred land with his Blue Coats, he kept the peace. Now the whites were on the warpath again, striking innocent camps in the night. It would be like the massacre on Sand Creek. There would be no peace. The Sioux must be ready to fight if they would not be slaughtered in the dark.

As was his habit, Sitting Bull went alone into the hills before making his decision. Then he came back and called his warriors about him.

"The soldiers have come shooting," he said. "They want war, so we will give it to them. We will not allow ourselves to be slaughtered like white men's cattle. We must stand together or they will kill us separately."

From the solemn-faced councilors came the cry, "Hau! Hau!" Then a rousing "Hopo! Hopo!"

Sitting Bull sent runners speeding to the four winds—to the agencies, to the camps of all the tribes, bearing news of the attack on Crazy Horse's village, bidding them all come to his camp on the Rosebud for a big council.

The Ogalalas found their welcome very pleasant at Sitting Bull's camp on Powder River. They were given food, lodges, robes, even pipes and kinnikinnick. There was also some ammunition for the guns Crazy Horse's warriors had taken from Fetterman's men. Indeed, Sitting Bull was surprisingly well supplied with guns and ammunition. He was clever about obtaining such things. He traded with the Slota, half-breeds from Canada, who were always well supplied. Also, he had set up a system of trading with the agency Indians. They would obtain guns and ammunition for hunting, bring them to Sitting Bull to trade for horses or robes, then go back and say the Dakotas had robbed them.

It seemed that spring would never come that year. Never had it been so late for the grass to grow green and the yellow and pink flowers to carpet the prairies, but at last the ice broke in the streams and the world was warm again.

The camps pushed slowly toward the Rosebud, taking time to allow the ponies to strengthen on the green grass. As they moved, more and more camps joined them until it was like small streams pouring into a big river. Even some of the No Clothes people joined them—that ill-fated band of Santees who had been chased from one part of the country to another ever since their big war in Minnesota.

As befitted his rank as chief of all the Sioux, and one of the older men, Sitting Bull rode at the head of the ever-growing column, and Crazy Horse, acknowledged war chief of all the Sioux, rode beside him. First came the Cheyennes, then the Ogalalas, followed by the Miniconjou. The Hunkpapas brought up the rear, taking the most dangerous position, as befitted their greater strength and importance. The Cheyennes sent their scouts ranging far ahead and the Hunkpapas kept scouts watching the rear.

Various travelers who joined the growing band brought reports of gatherings of the soldiers along the Yellowstone. They spoke of seeing Long Hair drilling his troops. A murmur ran through the band at the mention of the name Long Hair. They all knew him. He was the one who had opened the Thieves' Road into the Black Hills. He it was who killed many of their people to the south.

"Let the Long Hair come," Sitting Bull said calmly. "We are many. So long as we stand together they cannot kill us all."

CHAPTER FOURTEEN

"Soldiers Come Falling"

NEVER had the Indians been so happy. Any cloud of dread that may have hung over their spirits at the news of the gathering of the Blue Coats was dispelled by the knowledge of the strength of their own numbers. The circles of tipis stretched up the valley of the Rosebud for many miles. It was good to see so many of their people together in one place. That was as it should be, they decided. The hungry moons at the reservations were forgotten. The hunters had been fortunate. The squaws were making much meat. The drying racks were full. The pemmican sacks were bulging, the bubbling kettles were full of fat ribs or buffalo hump.

Every night there was feasting, dancing and visiting. Around the council fire sat the chiefs of all the tribes, Sitting Bull, Crazy Horse, Gall, Crow King, Black Moon, Two Moons, Old Bear, Spotted Eagle and Fast Bull.

It was in the bright time of the moon when the animals are fat that criers sped through the village spreading news that the great chief Sitting Bull was to give the Sun Dance. He had been to the hills to make medicine and had promised the Great Mystery to give the Sun Dance in gratitude for the Visions.

With song and ceremony, the Sun Dance pole was brought in to the grounds near the Deer Medicine Rocks. These separated cliff towers were a place of *Wakan* to the Sioux, for here it was the hunters paused to pray for success in the game hunt. Sitting Bull sat on a buffalo robe singing the Sun Dance song while two warriors cut fifty pieces of skin from his arms. Then he danced, gazing straight at the sun until it set. He faced the sun again at its rising and danced facing it, without food or water, until he fell as if dead.

Then he rose to his feet, spread his swollen arms to the sun and cried: "The Great Mystery has given me the Vision. I saw many Blue Coats falling into camp."

At this news the tom-toms beat faster and the prancing of the people increased in tempo.

Every day after the Sun Dance, Sitting Bull sent out scouts to watch for the Blue Coats. At last the grass and the game on the Rosebud were gone and the camp moved to Ash Creek, near the Little Big Horn.

Then, in the middle of the moon, the wolf call of the scouts echoed over the valley. It was the danger signal.

Soon they came galloping into camp, panting, "The

Three Star's soldiers are thick along the Rosebud. They are like the buffalo herds used to be."

Instantly the camp was in an uproar of shouts of "Hopo! Hurry! Hurry! Let us be off to kill the Blue Coats."

The young warriors could scarcely be restrained from dashing off instantly to count coup on the soldiers. Sitting Bull, however, had prepared for such an emergency by instructing his *Akicita* to keep them in camp.

Sitting Bull seldom made speeches but when he did his people listened to him. They remembered his Vision of many Blue Coats falling into camp. His medicine was good. Soon the shouting died down and the warriors listened.

"The Blue Coats are coming," the chief said. "They want war and we will give it to them. But it must be their sort of war, not ours. Their fast-shooting guns are many. Our guns are few and old. Many of us have only bows and arrows. We cannot fight the Blue Coats by dashing at them as we used to charge our enemies to count coups. This is not war for coup counting. It is war to kill soldiers so that they cannot kill us. For that purpose we must stay in a bunch. Shoot to kill and to get guns. Let the Blue Coats fire three times, then their new fast-firing guns will jam. That will be the time to kill them.

"Chief Crazy Horse is your war chief. Follow him. Do as he says. At daylight he will lead you out to drive off Three Star's soldiers. Then perhaps we can live in peace."

There were warriors from various tribes who went out with Crazy Horse, and young Jack Red Cloud, wearing a war bonnet, as befitted the son of a chief, was there eager to win his first glory in warfare and counteract the disgrace of his father's being an agency Indian.

They traveled all night and it was early morning when

they came in sight of Crook's camp. The older men advised stopping to rest the horses, but some of the young men were too eager to show how brave they were and it wasn't long before the fighting commenced.

Jack Red Cloud's horse was killed early in the battle. It was the Indian custom in such cases to pause and unhurriedly remove the bridle from the dead horse, thus displaying fearlessness in the face of danger. But Jack Red Cloud forgot how brave he intended to be and ran off as soon as his horse fell. Three Crow horsemen thereupon galloped after him, lashed him with their quirts and yanked off his war bonnet.

"You are only a girl," they taunted him. "You cannot wear a war bonnet. Why are you not at home with the squaws?"

And then young Jack Red Cloud completely disgraced himself forever. He burst into tears.

Crazy Horse almost succeeded in leading Crook's command into a natural trap called Dead Canyon. The General was, however, so badly mauled by Crazy Horse's men that he ordered a retreat up Goose Creek to Fort Meade. They ate their horses on the way—in a country teeming with game! But they were too afraid of the Indians to do any hunting.

Crazy Horse and Rain In The Face later said that if Crook had pushed on to join forces with Custer, he would have saved the day.

Sitting Bull was well pleased with the manner in which his advice to fight together rather than for individual honors had in the main been heeded. Since only half the Sioux were armed with guns, the rest only with bows and arrows, this was indeed a victory to talk about around the campfire, even though no scalps were taken. A few more guns had been obtained and these were coming to mean more to the Indians than scalps or coups.

The Moon When Animals Are Fat was in its wane that fateful day (June 25). It was hot and sultry. The sides of the tipis were rolled up to catch any stray breeze. The men leaned against the tipi poles and yawned or lay in the shade and dozed. The women plied awl or scraper listlessly.

There had been a big social dance the previous night. The young people were tired. Many of them were splashing in the river, swimming or having water fights. Children fished or waded in the stream. The herders tending the ponies back in the hills dozed over their task.

Since the defeat of Three Star's soldiers the Indians forgot Sitting Bull's Vision of many soldiers falling into camp. No one expected the Blue Coats to come this peaceful, lazy day.

Suddenly a Hunkpapa lad came dashing into camp, shouting at the top of his voice: "The soldiers are coming! I was out chasing horses. The Blue Coats dropped a pack. I picked it up. They are coming—"

Instantly the camp was in an uproar. Sitting Bull ran limping to the river bank and shaded his eyes with his hand, peering into the distance.

"Hoye!" he cried. "They are coming. I see the dust cloud—the Blue Coats."

He ran to get into his buckskin shirt fringed with bunches of hair, his high porcupine-trimmed moccasins, his trailing war bonnet of eagle feathers. He fastened his medicine sack around his neck, daubed red paint on his face.

His son, Crow Foot, came up leading his black war horse. Sitting Bull hastily painted a thunder bird and a crescent moon on its shoulders, seized his weapons and shield and then he was ready.

There was shooting in the upper part of the camp near the Cheyenne village. All the men were running to the west, yelling war cries.

Women were running around screaming and looking for their children and children were screaming for their mothers.

But there was one child of four snows who could not scream for his mother nor hear her calling him. It was John, Sitting Bull's deaf-and-dumb nephew, whom he had adopted. The terrified boy did not know what all the excitement was about. He ran this way and that crying silently until a bullet shot broke his leg. He crept into some bushes and was not found until the fighting was over.

Herders were running for the horses. Warriors were getting into war clothes and paint. Everything was confusion.

"Hurry! Hurry!" Sitting Bull urged. "But do not be thrown into a panic. Remember to fight together. To kill or be killed—not for coups."

Most of the young men who galloped to meet the soldiers were Sioux. The old men stayed back to cover the retreat of the women and children.

The fighting at the end of the camp was fierce. The Indians had not had much time to prepare for the attack, but they were holding ground; they hadn't been panicked.

The older men or leaders were not required to engage in battle, but Sitting Bull was right in the thick of it. Suddenly he pulled his black horse on its haunches, hardly able to believe what he saw. The Blue Coat leader was ordering his men to dismount! Then Sitting Bull knew

that the fighting for his side would be easy. If Reno's men
had remained mounted and had come charging into camp,
then the Indians would have been in trouble.

The Blue Coat chief acted frightened. He dashed this
way and that way as if he didn't know what to do. He ordered his men to fall back to the timber. The young warriors charged into them yelling their terrifying war whoops,
cutting the soldiers down with tomahawks or war clubs.
The Blue Coats did not have a chance on foot. The Indians
lay close to their ponies' necks and did not waste ammunition.

Then the soldiers' charge broke. They scrambled for
their horses and splashed pell-mell across the river, making
for the timber on a high bank.

The Indians galloped after them jeering, "You are
women. You should not be fighting. Go home to your
mothers."

Sitting Bull did not think it brave to kill such frightened
men. It would not be manly to count coup on them. His
heart was full of contempt for such fighting.

The soldiers scrambled to the top of a high steep hill.
The Indians swarmed all about them.

Some were making ready to try to attack the soldiers
on the hilltop. Then Sitting Bull became aware of excitement in the other end of the camp. He saw a cloud of
dust approaching, across the river.

"Hoye! Hoye!" Sitting Bull cried. "More Blue Coats!"

The Indians were melting away from Reno's position
to see what the excitement was about at the other end of
the camp.

Sitting Bull galloped through the villages. He arrived

at the other end in time to send a group of older men back
to hold Reno in check.

"Let Crazy Horse and his men take care of these horse
soldiers," he cried.

He himself remained to hold back the women who were
about to wade across the stream in the way of the warriors.
He must remain to see that the soldiers on the hill did not
charge into their rear. And if more Blue Coats came he
must be ready to deploy his men.

He saw the blue-coated horsemen come galloping along
a high ridge about two miles east of the Cheyenne camp.
There was the sound of bugles. Guidon were flapping. It
was a pretty sight.

The soldiers swerved off to a lower ridge and were riding
toward the ford. Four Cheyennes rode out to meet them.
Only four! The Blue Coats hesitated. Sitting Bull made
a clucking sound with his tongue at such poor fighting tac-
tics. Time and again he had seen his own people panicked
by a direct, bold charge. That was what he had been afraid
of. It was one reason he had remained behind. Now the
young warriors were out in full cry after the hesitant Blue
Coats.

One Bull went galloping into the stream. "Come along,"
he yelled to his uncle.

"There may be other Blue Coats coming," Sitting Bull
cried. He was uneasy. He had a feeling that there were
other soldiers coming. He was afraid all his men might be
drawn into the fight on the ridge. It might be an ambush.

Sitting Bull wanted to get into the fighting. It was hard
to remain behind to direct the actions. The Blue Coats
were completely surrounded by yelling Indians.

Most of them dismounted and went crawling up the numerous gullies that edged the ridge, or hid behind clumps of sagebrush. It was perfect terrain for the Sioux. Gradually they were creeping nearer and nearer. Most of them were firing arrows, which they could do from their hiding places, as the arrows would make a high arch before falling, whereas to fire guns the Indians would have to expose themselves. As it was, they could see the soldiers, but the soldiers could not see them.

Sitting Bull nodded with approval over the way his young men were fighting.

For a short time the sound of the firing on the ridge was deafening, then it grew less and less and finally ceased. Then the Indians swarmed over the ridge, yelling but not shooting. Someone shouted that all the Blue Coats were killed.

The sun was just past the middle when the fight ended and it had been past mid-morning when it commenced.

Sitting Bull rode to look over the battle ground. The stripped bodies gleamed white and sickly in the hot sun. It was over so quickly, but Sitting Bull's heart, made glad by the great victory, was also made heavy by the sound of the keening of the women for the Indian braves who had died.

Some of the warriors dressed in the soldiers' clothes they had taken before they went to pop away at the Blue Coats still hiding on the high place. There was no water up there and some of the Blue Coats tried to creep down a deep gulch and run across an open space to the stream, but they never got back. The Indians were waiting for them to try this very thing.

The Indians got much loot from the soldiers slain on

the ridge. There was much green paper which seemed valueless and was thrown away. One man found some round metal pieces. He was told that these could be used at the trading posts to obtain guns and ammunition.

The weapons and cartridges of the slain soldiers were eagerly gathered. One of the Indians was mystified by a round metal thing he took from one of the soldiers.

He heard a ticking sound and held it to his ear. "It is alive!" he cried. The other Sioux gathered around to see and listen to this strange bit of white man's medicine. They were eager to trade for it but the young man wished to keep it for himself. The next day he was disappointed to find that it had "died" during the night. It no longer made the ticking sound.

Many of the Indians got soldiers' saddles. These were highly prized treasures. Yellow Weasel picked up a bugle, but couldn't get a sound from it.

Many fine horses were captured and these were distributed among the fighters.

Some of the young men were still popping away at the Blue Coats in the timber, but no organized charge was made.

"Wait, they will come out for water," the old men said. "We can get them then and not lose our men and waste our ammunition."

The camps were being moved. It was customary when deaths had taken place in a village to move on to another location. The Indian women who had lost sons or husbands in the battle dressed themselves in rags, let their hair hang loose, blackened their faces and gashed their arms and legs to show their grief.

Although the big victory dance would not be held until

four days had passed, there were several small dances by the young men who could not restrain themselves. But Sitting Bull's heart was still heavy in the midst of all the rejoicing. He had lived long and acquired wisdom not possessed by the young warriors. They had wiped out the Blue Coat command on the ridge. Yes. But there would be more and more Blue Coats. It was like trying to check a flood with a handful of mud.

The heart of the Great Father would now be bad—very bad against his red children. He would send more and more Blue Coats to destroy them—or worse, bring them onto the hated reservations.

"It is better to die fighting than to starve to death," Sitting Bull often told his warriors. This would always be his advice. Life on the reservations was worse than death, he thought. He and his people would now be hounded to the four corners of the earth, he knew, but it would be best to die fighting, as befitted an Indian brave. Only the woman-hearted gave up to become agency loafers.

CHAPTER FIFTEEN

No Place to Rest

THE following day the victory-flushed Indians charged Reno's force on the bluff. During the night, however, the men had dug deep trenches for themselves. Sitting Bull was with the attacking Sioux, but his heart was not in the battle. A number of his people had died in the battle yesterday. Others were dying today. It would be ever thus. He knew that if he ordered the Indians to attack from all sides of the bluff at once, Reno's men could all be wiped out as the others had been. But that would inflame the Great Father's heart even more. And he would send the Blue Coats like a mighty flood. There was no end to them. No, the Sioux must travel on and on and whenever they were pushed into a corner they must turn and fight. This they must do until they died.

So the fighting against the soldiers on the bluff was without leadership. And the Indians were weary from their battle of the previous day.

"Wait," some of the weary ones advised. "They are well dug in. We will lose good ammunition and men. There is no water up there. Soon they will go to the stream and we will rub them out."

Soon, however, the mirror flashes from a far hill told that another large company of Blue Coats was coming up the river with wagon guns.

"Scatter to the four winds in little groups," Sitting Bull sent word through the camp. "That way it will be harder for the soldiers to find us. Get guns and ammunition and some day soon we will gather again."

Many of the tipis were already down. By the time Terry's army reached the terrible scene of the Custer Massacre the Indians had scattered like wind-driven leaves and there was no single trail to follow.

Sitting Bull had a difficult time making the Indians stay scattered. They felt safer near him and kept flocking to his camp. Also many more from the agencies came to join him. From them he learned that every day new battalions of horse soldiers, of walking soldiers, of wagon guns were being brought in from all the forts along the Missouri.

It was from them that he learned that the white chief of the soldiers killed on the ridge had been none other than Custer, the one they called "Long Hair." But he had cut his long, yellow hair off before the battle, so no one had recognized him. He was the one who had slain many Indians in the land to the south. He was the one who had opened the Thieves' Road into the Sioux' sacred Black

Hills country. Sitting Bull could not find it in his heart to be sorry that such an enemy had been slain. But it was not until then that he or any of his people knew who the leader of the wiped-out command had been.

Curly, the Indian scout with the Custer band who was the only one to escape, told of the talk Long Hair had had with him. He told the story at the agency and the agency Indians carried it to Sitting Bull's ears. Long Hair had not done what he had been told to do. Three columns of Blue Coats were to strike the camp on the Rosebud at once. But Long Hair had been eager for personal glory. The Great Father's heart was bad against him; he was in disgrace. So he hoped to strike the Indian villages first and conquer them himself. Then he, himself, would undoubtedly be the chief of all the whites—the Great Father.

Sitting Bull nodded. He could not but give Long Hair his grudging admiration. Here was a brave man who fought as the Indians did—for personal glory.

Sitting Bull called a council of his leaders.

"The white men are all around us," he said. "We are like a small herd of buffaloes in the middle of a surround. We can stay and be chased from one camp to another and be killed, or we can escape to the land of the Grandmother (Canada) and live at peace."

"That is the coward's way," Crazy Horse cried. "I will live the life of the warrior. I choose to remain."

"You will remain to be penned up on a reservation like the white man's cow, then," Sitting Bull said scornfully. "There is no other way. The white men are too many. We cannot fight them forever. Our ammunition is low now. Since the Long Hair's death we will not be allowed to get any more. We can live in peace and freedom in the land of the Grandmother. There will be no peace or freedom ever for us here."

"We all must die," Crazy Horse cried. "I will die fighting. Not like a woman."

"When I die, it will be fighting, too," Sitting Bull said quietly. "But now the women and children and the aged must be cared for. I will take them to the land of the Grandmother."

And so the two great leaders parted, Sitting Bull to move northward with his band; Crazy Horse to go to the Big Horns.

The Red Coats in Canada agreed to allow Sitting Bull and his people to remain in the land of the Grandmother so long as they did not make trouble. There were no buffalo in Canada, however, so the Sioux had to go south to hunt. It was in the season of Making Meat that runners brought the news to Sitting Bull's camp on the Grand River that the Blue Coats were attacking the camp at Slim Buttes.

Sitting Bull stripped to the breechclout, painted his face red, put on his Strong Heart bonnet with the two horns and the feather streamer in back, leaped on his black war horse and, calling his warriors together, rode to the rescue.

Once more the treacherous "Grabber" had led the enemy to a Sioux camp. Many were the times Sitting Bull wished he had let his men kill him out there on the trail. And how different was the case of Little Assiniboin, who was truly as a brother to Sitting Bull.

The soldiers at Slim Buttes were so numerous that all Sitting Bull's men could do was fire at them and drive them away. But they were lucky to do that. There were no coups that day and it was a sorrowful sight that met Sitting Bull's eyes in the Slim Buttes camp, for women and children had been shot down as they tried to run away from the soldiers' guns.

Sitting Bull went back to his hunting after the dead were buried but there was no peace for him. It was in the Moon When The Elks Shed Their Antlers (November), that the news was brought to him that the Sioux holy land, the Black Hills, was being sold.

"But that cannot be!" he cried. "The Great Father promised it would never be sold until three out of every four sign."

"But the other chiefs have signed the paper," the messenger said.

At first Sitting Bull thought that the chiefs had been given the white man's fire water. Then he learned that Red Tail and Spotted Tail and others had been put inside the stockade at the fort and then the "agreement" was read to them saying that all their land was being "sold" and they would be sent to the South Country.

At first they refused to sign. The South Country was hated by the northern Indians. They wanted to stay on their own lands. But the agent said that their children would not be fed until they signed, so finally they signed away part of the holy land of their fathers.

All that Sitting Bull could do when he heard this last bit of news was put his head in his hands and groan. Was there never to be an end to the treachery of the palefaces? His heart was growing so big with hatred for them that it seemed as if it must burst from the pressure.

The next thing the soldiers did was to send "Bear Coat," General Miles, to make a fort on the Yellowstone at the mouth of the Tongue River. First the Black Hills were taken and now the Big Horns country was being threatened. Sit-ting Bull attacked Bear Coat's wagon train, getting many mules, but the wagons went clattering down the river, belching fire. Sitting Bull then had Big Leggins, a half-breed with his band, write a note he dictated and place it in a forked stick in the trail. It said:

"Yellowstone.
"I want to know what you are doing on this road. You scare all the buffalo away. I want to hunt in this place. I want you to turn back from here. If you don't, I will fight you again. I want you to leave what you have got here and turn back from here.

"I am your friend
"Sitting Bull
"I mean all the rations you have got and some powder. Wish you would write me as soon as you can."

Little wonder that the white men called Sitting Bull "in-solent."

Not long after this two Hunkpapa Indians from Standing Rock agency came to Sitting Bull's lodge saying that Bear Coat had a message for him. He would like to have him come to his camp for a powwow.

Sitting Bull called his important men together for a council. Finally it was agreed that the chief should take two hundred warriors and ride to Bear Coat's camp to see what he had to say.

When the Hunkpapas reached the camp there was some talking back and forth about who should go to whose lines for the parley. Sitting Bull certainly had no reason to trust any white man and General Miles did not display any great eagerness to put himself at the Indians' mercy, even though his soldiers had a Gatling gun pointed at them.

At length Sitting Bull settled the argument by suggesting that they meet midway between the lines, both leaving guns behind. This was done.

Sitting Bull, with four of his warriors, went midway of the field; Miles likewise came out with four men and they all sat facing each other. Miles writes that Sitting Bull was "a fine, powerful, intelligent, determined-looking man" and that his manner was "cold, but dignified and courteous."

Miles said, "Sitting Bull, you have always been against the white men."

Sitting Bull replied, "All I want is food for my people and to be let alone. It is the white men who start the fighting every time."

General Miles went on talking persuasively for some time trying to convince Sitting Bull of the advantages of coming on to the agency. Sitting Bull harped on the same old theme—that he wanted to be left alone in the country the Great Father had promised him. He wanted the Black Hills and the Big Horns country. He wanted no whites on his land.

The General had trouble keeping his temper. He complained that "Sitting Bull spoke like a conqueror and looked like one."

The council broke up when Sitting Bull cried, "No Indian that ever lived loved the white man, and no white man that ever lived loved the Indian. God Almighty made me an Indian and not agency Indian, and I do not intend to become one."

The next day another meeting was held. Bear Coat again put forth his arguments and Sitting Bull chanted his old refrain and wound up by telling the general that all white men were liars, which put Miles into a rage. He shouted that he would give Sitting Bull fifteen minutes to go back to his lines and get ready to fight. Sitting Bull did not understand this order—perhaps the interpreter garbled it. Anyway, the soldiers fired, taking the Hunkpapas by surprise.

There was a lively skirmish during which one Indian was killed. The Sioux set fire to the prairie, but the grass was short and green and the horse soldiers galloped through it to scatter the Hunkpapas, who fled to the timber. Miles captured the Sioux camp and all of the meat supply.

Sitting Bull went searching for Crazy Horse, hoping to join forces with him, but was unable to find him because the soldiers dogged his footsteps and jumped his camp every time he settled down. At last he led his band back to Canada where he hoped they would be allowed to live in peace.

CHAPTER SIXTEEN

In the Land of the Grandmother

FOR a time Canada seemed like a haven of peace to the hectored Sioux. The Red Coats came to Sitting Bull and told him that he and his people would be allowed to remain in the country unmolested so long as they behaved themselves. But there must be no raiding, no horse stealing.

The chief agreed to these stipulations. For a time the Sioux camp lived in peace and harmony, but after a while the young warriors began to chafe at the inactivity. This sort of life was all right for old men with aching joints

141

but how were the young men to earn their eagle feathers, win coups, merely by hunting or lounging around camp? Some of the older ones, too, grew dissatisfied because of the scarcity of food and talked of going back to the reserva-tion.

This talk, however, was stopped abruptly when Bear Leggins came to visit the Sitting Bull camp and told of the fate of Crazy Horse. He and his people likewise had been driven from corner to corner. During the Moon of The Terrible Cold, Miles' horse soldiers had attacked the Cheyenne camp just before dawn. They were right in the middle of the village, taking it by surprise. The Indians swarmed from their tipis naked; they had not time to dress. They clambered up a canyon and scattered to hide from the troops as best they could. The cold was terrible. Even the hardy Cheyennes, many of them, could not withstand it. Twelve babies froze to death that first night.

Bear Leggins was sitting beside the campfire surrounded by Sitting Bull's people. A sound of pity and horror rippled through the crowd at these details.

Bear Leggins went on to tell how some of the children had been saved when the men killed the horses, disem-boweled them and thrust the children into the cavities. The starving, freezing Cheyennes sought out Crazy Horse's camp where they were given food and clothing from the Sioux' scanty supplies. Most of them surrendered at the agency. A few remained with Crazy Horse to be hounded from place to place until he, too, surrendered.

"I was sent to Crazy Horse, myself," Bear Leggins cried. "With the white man's message. I delivered it in good faith. I was not to blame. Crazy Horse was to be made the great leader over all the Indians. He would be given much honor. He could do as he pleased. It was the agent's promise."

"White man's promise!" Sitting Bull spat out the words with contempt.

Bear Leggins nodded and went on to tell the rest of the story—of how Crazy Horse had not been made a great chief at all—had in fact been a virtual prisoner. Of how he wanted to take his wife who was gravely ill with the white man's coughing sickness to her own people for medical treatment. The request was refused and Crazy Horse took her anyway. He wasn't running away. He came back of his own accord and was immediately arrested. He resisted and was stabbed in the back.

Silence hung like a heavy cloud over Sitting Bull's camp for some time after Bear Leggins finished his story. For some considerable time there was no more talk of anyone's going back to the reservation.

The Red Coats had said that there must be no horse stealing. The Indians had been taught that horse stealing was brave and commendable. It was second nature to them. Now suddenly they must stop. Nevertheless there was only one instance of the Indian's favorite pastime during Sitting Bull's stay in Canada. That time, although it was Sitting Bull's own brother-in-law who was one of the guilty ones, the chief dealt so severely with the culprits that there was no repetition.

It was in the Moon of Falling Leaves, 1878, that a haggard, bedraggled Indian staggered into camp. It was Crow Feather, a Nez Percé Indian who could speak the Sioux language. He gasped out a terrible story of how his people under chief Joseph had been driven from their homes and chased thousands of miles by General Miles. Now they were trapped at Bear Paw Mountains. More than half his force had been slain. Would Sitting Bull bring his warriors and come to chief Joseph's aid?

Sitting Bull's heart was torn. The Nez Percés were ancient enemies but that was forgotten now. All redskins were friends against the common foe. Every instinct of his being made him yearn to rush to Joseph's aid. But he could not do that. He had given his promise to the Red Coats to keep the peace. His people would be driven from Canada if he broke his pledge.

He spread his hands in a helpless gesture. "Go back to Joseph," he said hopelessly. "Tell him I cannot go to help him. It is useless. My people would be made to suffer—and for nothing. Tell Joseph to bring his people here. They will be safe from the Blue Coats, and then I will help them."

A few battered, haggard Nez Percés did get through to Sitting Bull's camp. But the noble chief Joseph gave up—surrendered finally, ending one of the greatest stands in history. With fewer than three hundred warriors he had stood off five thousand soldiers. He had led his people through enemy country for two thousand miles. Again and again he defeated the nation's best soldiers. When stopped he was only thirty miles from his goal—the Canada border. It was one of the greatest marches of all time.

Chief Joseph's daughter was one of the pitiful group that got to Sitting Bull's camp. While she sobbed out the story of that terrible trek, Sitting Bull thought his heart could not stand the pressure of hate against the white men.

It was only a few weeks later and while the sufferings of Crazy Horse and the Nez Percés were still fresh in his mind

that Sitting Bull was sent for to come to the Red Coat's
fort to talk with General Terry.

"Why should I talk with Star Terry?" Sitting Bull cried.
"The white men are all liars."

Nevertheless, the Mounted Police Commissioner finally
persuaded Sitting Bull to accompany him to Fort Walsh.
The chief, however, did not deem the occasion important
enough to don any finery. He wore a wolfskin cap, a black
calico shirt with white polka dots, and a red blanket over
his shoulders.

When they reached Fort Walsh Sitting Bull stopped like
a balky mule and refused to go inside. It took the entire
force of Red Coats, courteously promising protection, to
induce the chief and his party to go within.

Terry rose to give in a patronizing tone the Great Father's message. He was willing to forgive the Sioux if they
would come to the reservation.

Sitting Bull rose up in all his wrath. His voice thundered
through the room and, as he spoke, Terry and his aides
looked as if they could shrivel up and become invisible.

"Why should the Great Father forgive *us?*" he demanded. "What treaty that the whites have made has the
red man broken? What treaty that the whites ever made
with us red men have they kept? When I was a boy the
Sioux owned the world. The sun rose and set in their
lands. Where are our lands? Who stole them? Who slew our
warriors and our women and children? What white man
can say I ever stole his lands? What does the Great Father
have to forgive me for?"

Terry then took a more conciliatory tone, saying that
Sitting Bull's band was the only one that had not sur-

rendered; that it would be best for his people if he went to the reservation, giving up his horses and arms in exchange for cattle.

Sitting Bull's reply was scornful. "For sixty-four snows you have kept at me and my people and treated us bad. What have we done that you wish us to stop? We have done nothing. It is all the people on your side who have started us to do as we did. We could not go any place else so we came here. I would like to know why you come here? I did not give you that country; but you followed me about, so I had to leave and come over to this country. You have got ears, and eyes to see with, and you see how I live with these people. You see me. Here I am. You come here to tell us lies, but we don't want to hear them. I don't wish any such language used to me. I intend to stay here and raise this country full of grown people. That is enough, so no more. The part of the country you gave me, you ran me out of. I don't want to hear two more words. I wish you to go back."

He paused for breath. He was a plain, unhandsome man in shabby attire, but there emanated from him now that inner force with which he often impressed people. Then he added to his speech the stinger that reddened Terry's cheeks.

"Tell them in Washington," he said, "that if they have one man who speaks the truth to send him to me and I will listen. I don't believe in a government that has made fifty-two treaties with the Sioux and has kept none of them."

After delivering this whiplash of scorn he threw his blanket over his shoulder and stalked from the room.

The meeting had been an uncomfortable one for Terry. Although he was undoubtedly a believer in the theory that "the only good Indian was a dead Indian," he could not possibly fail to see the justice of the chief's remarks.

The air had been electric between them. It was Terry who had been in command of the troops when Custer's force was wiped out. It was hardly within the limitations of human nature that he could have any kindness in his heart for Sitting Bull, and the knowledge must have rankled in his mind that he with thousands of fine, well-equipped soldiers had not been able to keep the Sioux in check, while a handful of Canadian Mounted Police were doing so without shedding a drop of blood.

So Terry had to return and report the failure of his mission.

Life in Canada, however, was not too easy. The government promised the Sioux refuge but refused to feed them. There were no buffalo except south of the border. The young men went across to hunt but were continuously hectored by Bear Coat's soldiers. Then Dakota became populated by settlers and the buffalo disappeared. So long as Sitting Bull had large piles of shaggy buffalo hides to barter he could get guns, ammunition, horses, food and other supplies from the traders but when there was no more hunting stark poverty and starvation stared the Sitting Bull band in the face.

Gall, who had always been jealous of Sitting Bull's power, and Crow King stirred up dissatisfaction among the men and induced a large number to follow them to the agency. Sitting Bull was left with but a remnant of his force and these were mainly old people and children, who were hungry and ragged.

The pressure on the chief was relentless. A reward was offered to the man who would bring him in. The traders.

who had been mainly responsible for keeping him in Canada in the first place, lost interest in him. A new commissioner replaced Walsh, who had been friendly to him. Obviously, Sitting Bull had worn out his welcome in Canada.

Relentless fate was piling circumstance on circumstance. One of Sitting Bull's daughters ran away with an agency Indian. The report was brought back that he had deserted her and that she was in the jail at Fort Yates. His people were hungry. They were homesick. They were lonely. The Canadians were pressing him to go to the agency.

At last the weight was too much. He had done all that he could for his people. No doubt they would be happier on the reservation. He went to the one Canadian trader he liked and trusted and said that he was giving himself up. The trader could take him and his people in and collect the reward.

Sitting Bull fully expected to be killed when he went in. "Accidents" had happened to Crazy Horse, to Spotted Tail, to Chief Joseph, to Dull Knife. It was too much to expect that he, who had caused the Blue Coats so much trouble, who had been the last of all to surrender, should fare more fortunately. But the old people would be better off, he thought, as he rode in to Fort Buford on July 19, 1881, to give himself up, voluntarily. He had finally surrendered, not to the might of the white man, but to hunger.

CHAPTER SEVENTEEN

Still a Chief

IT WAS a bitter moment in the proud chief's life when he had to walk into the fort past the line of curious officers and soldiers. He thought he saw gloating in the eyes of some of them over his downfall. His face was lined and

151

haggard; his clothes worn and shabby. He walked with a limp. There was nothing imposing-looking about him.

He handed his weapons to his eight-year-old boy, Crow Foot, to give to the officers, saying: "My son, if you live, you will never be a man in this world, because you can never have a pony or a gun."

It seemed to him very sad that his own boy must grow up to be like a white man—could never know the joys of Indian life. That sort of thing was gone forever.

His main concern now was to find out about his daughter who, he heard, had been imprisoned. When he was assured that she was free, safe and well, some of the lines eased from his face.

Sitting Bull had been promised that when he gave up his weapons he would be "pardoned," fed and given a place of his own to live in. Instead, he was arrested for being the killer of Custer and sent to Fort Randall.

He had expected something of the sort and was surprised only that they hadn't found some excuse to kill him right away. Life at Fort Randall, however, was not too bad. The officers respected him and treated him like a chief. He remained a prisoner for two years and was then allowed to go where his people were at Standing Rock Reservation. He settled on the Grand River, near his birthplace.

He expected, of course, to go on being chief of the Sioux at the agency, but he was soon to learn that his battle for his rights was far from over.

The moment he stepped into the office of the agent, "White Hair," Major James McLaughlin, he felt a wave of antagonism hit him, and he stiffened, instinctively, resentful against it.

He had been treated fairly at Fort Randall and as a result of such treatment his heart had commenced to soften toward the whites. He entered the agent's office in a spirit of friendliness. Now here was the old feeling of mistrust back again. He knew right away that things would never be right between himself and McLaughlin. The agent did not like him. He was afraid. He feared Sitting Bull's power and would try to undermine him.

Before the interview was over McLaughlin made it plain that he did not consider Sitting Bull a chief, and it was not long before Bull discovered that Gall had managed to work himself into the agent's good graces and he and John Grass were being treated like chiefs, although Gall, who agreed with everything White Hair said, was the agent's favorite.

Sitting Bull, however, wasn't much concerned. He knew that his power with his people was still strong so it mattered little whether White Hair considered him a chief or not. The Sioux still came to him for advice; he was the leader of the councils. Let Gall fawn upon the white man like a yellow dog; Sitting Bull was still confident of his power.

McLaughlin was to learn that it took more than a nod from him to make a man a chief. A commission had been sent to "investigate" the scandalous manner in which the sale of the Black Hills had been imposed upon the Sioux. The Senate Committee sent to investigate the disgraceful circumstances was composed of men who had little interest in the Indian problem and absolutely no understanding of Indian ways. It was to be many years before the whole disgraceful matter would be brought to light and attempts made to make amends. But by that time it was too late to benefit the Indians who had been injured.

The Senate Committee wanted to get the matter finished and a pretty report made to be filed away some place in

Washington. McLaughlin appointed John Grass to act as chief. John became bewildered by the barrage of questions fired at him. He tried to tell the committee members that the signing of the agreement of '82 was an acciden . They had been threatened, confused—

"But you did sign," a committeeman roared. "You didn't have to sign—"

Sitting Bull thereupon stood up and remained standing until the chairman of the meeting was forced to recognize him.

Grudgingly the chairman said to the interpreter, "Ask Sitting Bull if he has anything to say to the committee."

Sitting Bull replied, "Of course I will speak if you desire me to do so. I suppose it is *only* such men as you desire to speak who must say anything."

The chairman said gruffly, "We supposed the Indians would select men to speak for them. But any man who desires to speak, or any man the Indians here desire to talk for them, we shall be glad to hear if he has anything to say."

"Do you know who I am that you speak as you do?" Sitting Bull asked quietly, but there was a dangerous gleam in his eye.

"I know," snapped the chairman, "that you are Sitting Bull, and if you have anything to say, we shall be glad to hear you."

"Do you recognize me?" insisted the old chief. "Do you know who I am?"

"I know you are Sitting Bull." The committeeman was becoming irritated. He came to question, not to be questioned.

"You say I am Sitting Bull, but do you know what position I hold?"

"I do not recognize any difference between you and the other Indians at this agency."

"I am here," Sitting Bull said mildly, "by the will of the Great Spirit and by His will I am a chief. My heart is red and sweet, and I know it is sweet because whatever passes near me puts out its tongue to me; and yet you men have come here to talk with us and you say you do not know who I am. I want to tell you that if the Great Spirit has chosen anyone to be the chief of this country, it is myself."

The pompous Congressman acting as chairman looked as if he were about to explode with anger at this arrogant redskin's attempt to put him in his place and McLaughlin's face was crimson.

The chairman lost all his dignity as he shouted, "What rubbish you talk! Chiefs are not appointed by God. McLaughlin told me John Grass and Gall were the Sioux leaders here."

Then a crafty, half-smile crossed Sitting Bull's face. He waved his hand and the Sioux arose and in a body left the room. McLaughlin could appoint his favorite yes-men as so-called chiefs, but Sitting Bull's power over his people still held, whether the white men acknowledged him or not. So the meeting got nowhere. The Congressmen would not acknowledge that God had anything to do with making Sitting Bull a chief. They did not consider him one and that seemed to settle the matter in their minds. The committeemen had come to Standing Rock with the belief that all Indians were thieves and beggars. They considered the government very kind to issue them meager rations. They were not very eager to have their minds changed, so they did nothing at all to get at the root of the matter.

"Sitting Bull is a troublemaker," they said. McLaughlin

agreed with them and redoubled his systematic efforts to break Bull's power. Gall and John Grass were shoved into prominence at every opportunity; yet the Sioux still flocked to Sitting Bull's cabin for advice. To them he was still their chief. Naturally this state of affairs created an almost in· tolerable situation.

McLaughlin, therefore, eagerly seized the opportunity of getting rid of his problem for a season, when Colonel Allen took the old chief on a tour of exhibition through the cities of the East, advertising him as "General Custer's slayer." This crowning indignity, being made a side-show spectacle, was authorized by the Secretary of the Interior.

The next year Sitting Bull was passed on as a similar attraction to Buffalo Bill's Wild West Show. Here he was happier than he had been with Colonel Allen's exhibition, for Buffalo Bill was friendly, understanding and "spoke with the straight tongue," thus winning Bull's respect. The chief's inborn kindliness and generosity came to the surface among these people who lived like a large, happy family under their big-hearted "boss," Buffalo Bill Cody.

Sitting Bull adopted Annie Oakley, the girl sharpshooter with the show, as his daughter. Around the camp his favorite costume consisted of a brocaded velvet waistcoat, trousers with a big flower design, a red necktie, his shirt tail hanging out, and always the large crucifix Father De Smet had given him. With this outlandish costume he wore beaded moccasins.

He hated the times he had to parade around the arena in crimson tunic and trailing eagle-feather headdress. The public believed him to be an arch villain and Custer's slayer and they hissed him at every appearance. However, his autographs, which he learned to scrawl, sold like hot cakes for a dollar apiece. Nevertheless, his money was always gone almost as soon as it hit his pockets for he gave it away to the numerous newsboys and street urchins who clambered around his tent.

He assumed a ferocious expression for the benefit of his audiences but the more he saw of white people, the more his contempt for them grew. Their silly, meaningless everlasting talk annoyed him. Their greediness and poor manners made him wish for the kindly, generous atmosphere of the tipi and the gentle courtesy of his people.

At first the Wild West Show was exciting. It made his blood run fast as in the old days of the buffalo hunt or the pony-stealing raids—the thunder of hoofs, the crack of rifles, the shouts, the smell of horses, aroused old memories. There was the pony race between Indian boys, just as it had been on the plains; the race between a boy on foot and one on horseback; the Pony Express rider; the attack on the Deadwood Mail Coach. All those seemed real, but Sitting Bull had to smile at the scene of the capture and torture to death of a scout by a Plains Indian. The Plains Indians did not torture victims, but the whites liked to believe they did.

Buffalo Bill arranged for an interview for him with the press. He was questioned about his part in the Custer battle. He said, "Nobody knew who killed Custer; everybody fired at him. Custer was a brave warrior but made a mistake. The Indians honored him and did not scalp him. I fought for my people. My people said I was right. I will answer to my people. I will answer for the dead of my people. Let the palefaces do the same on their side."

He was taken to Washington to shake hands with the Great White Father. He was unimpressed by the Great

Father, but the large buildings and the crowds of people awed him.

"I wish I had known this when I was a boy," he was heard to murmur. "The white people are so many that if every Indian in the West killed one every step he took, the dead would not be missed among you."

Later he said, "I go back to my people in one more moon. I will tell them what I have seen. They will never go on the warpath again. I have learned much. Indian must keep quiet or die. The Great Father must protect us and give us justice."

He was weary and wanted to return to his home. He said to Buffalo Bill, "The tipi is a better place for the red man. I am tired of houses and noise. Everywhere I go white people point fingers and make faces of hate at me. White men talk too much. To my ears it is like the noise of waters which man cannot stop."

Buffalo Bill gave Sitting Bull a fine white horse as a present when he returned to the reservation.

CHAPTER EIGHTEEN

"My People Need Me"

SITTING BULL was not happy upon the reservation yet he tried to make the best of matters. He was with his family and his people were around him. If the old ways of life were doomed it was the old people and the young men who had had a taste of Indian life who would suffer. He supposed it would not matter much to the children who were reared to live the white man's way. They would not know the difference.

What made the old ones unhappiest was that the agents forbade the Indian dancing, their songs, their painting on hides, their handwork. It was very hard for the old people

to give up the accustomed ways of life for ones so un-
familiar to them. It was hard to learn to use new foods. The
agents issued sacks of four. The squaws, never having used
it, had no idea what to do with it except dump the flour on
the ground and cut holes in the sacks and use them for
shirts for their children. The bacon was issued in slabs.
The squaws tried stewing the piece in a kettle like a piece
of buffalo meat and thought it very poor sort of food,
indeed.

It made Sitting Bull almost weep to see his children
come home from school with their hair cut off short. He
feared that this practice would make the hair sprout out
on their faces as it did on the white man's. He wanted his
children to go to school, though. He told them many times
that they must learn to read the white man's marks and
numbers to keep from being cheated. Yet he disliked the
schools and churches because they scattered the mother
force. Contrary to the white man's notion, Indian women
did exert great influence in the tribe because they were
the source of all Indian learning to their children. From
their mothers the boys and girls learned to love nature;
they learned their religion, all the Indian lore. Now the
schools and churches took over things of this nature, leaving the mother influence very weakened.

He returned from his trip with Buffalo Bill fully con-
vinced that open hostility against the white man was useless. There was one thing, however, that aroused him to
open action: the re-establishment of the religion of his
fathers. His people were falling more and more under the
influence of the white missionaries and he didn't like it.

"Why should you listen to them?" he cried. "They cannot agree among themselves about the right manner of

worship. Each missionary shouts that his way is the right way; then they quarrel among themselves about it. None of them ever goes out alone to meet the Great Mystery. That is the way it is done. Not by gathering in groups and shouting from pulpits."

To Sitting Bull religion meant kinship with all living things and through them unity with the One Above. Religion was a beautiful, real and living function—a part of every-day existence, not just a Sunday affair.

Mary Collins, a missionary of the Congregational Church, established a mission about ten miles from Sitting Bull's camp. He tried hard to keep his people from yielding to her influence. Other than trying to keep his friends from her mission he ignored her until one day when one of his neighbor's children was seriously ill. The man brought the baby to Sitting Bull to cure. He tried all his charms but nothing would work. He saw the child was about to die, and jumping on a horse he carried it to Mary Collins' house.

"Missionary Woman, come out!" he cried.

Mary Collins was an independent little person. She was not in the habit of jumping like a squaw at some Indian's command. Not even if he were a chief. She made Sitting Bull come to her.

He placed the child in her lap and begged her to heal it if she could. Perhaps her medicine was better than his.

The child was in convulsions, but she lanced its blackened gums, bathed it, applied some simple remedy and it fell into peaceful slumber.

"Mary Collins," Sitting Bull said ceremoniously, "I adopt you as my daughter."

This was the highest tribute the chief could pay.

Mary Collins smiled up at him. "Thank you, father," she said. "I understand you have already adopted eleven youngsters on the reservation besides your own and they all revere you. If I'm to be your daughter, I'll expect you to come to church."

Sitting Bull backed toward the door. "No," he said. "I will not come into your church. The One Above did not intend His children to worship indoors. He intends them to meet Him face-to-face outdoors and alone."

For ten years the two remained good friends, though rivals.

Mary Collins put forth strenuous efforts to convert Sitting Bull. It would have been quite a triumph for her if she could have brought him into her fold. But he indignantly denied that his soul needed saving. He felt in complete harmony with the *Wakan Tanka*.

"I do not lie. I do not cheat. I do not take lands or anything else that does not belong to me. I give food and help to everyone who comes to me. Is that what your man called Jesus told men to do? Yet how many whites follow His teaching?" Sitting Bull was sure that Jesus had a white heart and spoke with the straight tongue. It was highly wicked of the whites to nail such a good man to the cross.

Mary Collins got exactly nowhere with the chief.

A rivalry of a different sort and not so friendly was going on upon the reservation—that between Gall and Sitting Bull for power. Gall still held the favor of McLaughlin and he had his followers. There were always plenty who sought extra privileges or rations by standing in well with the agent.

Gall now was not above trying to undermine Sitting Bull

by saying that he was a coward—that he had no more courage than could be put on a fingernail.

Sitting Bull didn't get excited by such remarks. His people knew that he was no coward. That was all that mattered.

There was one thing that annoyed him, though. It was
the way the Indian police McLaughlin appointed strutted
around as if they owned the universe. The Sioux *Akicita*
had been sensible fellows. They were members of the Fox
Warrior Society who won their position by bravery in battle. They knew how to keep order and managed to do it
without raising a lot of resentment, but McLaughlin picked
the policemen from what he called the "good boys," the
ones who came around licking his boots, in other words.
There was Bull Head, for instance. McLaughlin made him
an officer and he immediately got so conceited that he became unendurable, swaggering around in his brass-but-
toned, blue uniform, shouting orders even to those older
than he.

Sitting Bull's medicine was still good. A number of times
he foretold what the weather would be for the coming
season, as he did the terrible summer of 1889 when no rain
fell and the sun burned up the crops. He planted no crops
himself that year, for he knew they would fail from lack
of moisture. In spite of the dreadful heat, some of his
people sneaked away from the watchful eye of the agent
to hold the Sun Dance in an effort to win back the favor
of the Great Spirit. They suffered so from heat and thirst
during the dance that Sitting Bull's heart ached for them.

"I will bring the rain to give you relief," he said.

He went to the hills for a time of communion with the

Great Mystery, then came to where his people were, waved his blanket and placed it on the ground three times, then sat down to wait. In a very short time clouds began to float over the heretofore brassy sky, a cool breeze sprang up and soon raindrops as big as dimes were dancing over the parched land.

There are a number of such instances on record of Sitting Bull's power to control the weather.

Mary Collins, the missionary, sniffed when she heard these stories. "That old humbug pagan!" she cried. "He is such a child of nature that he senses in advance what the weather will be, then he goes through his hocus-pocus to make his people believe that he controls the weather!"

The rivalry between the chief and the missionary as to whose "medicine" was stronger still persisted. And there was still no let-up in the efforts of McLaughlin to break the influence of the man he hated and feared. He welcomed every opportunity to get Sitting Bull off the reservation, he urged the chief to accept Buffalo Bill's invitation to go to England with his show, but the chief refused, saying simply, "My people need me." As well they did!

In 1888 the Commission came to Standing Rock agency proposing to buy eleven million acres of the best of the Sioux lands, leaving, of course, the poorest land for the Indians. And they offered fifty cents an acre for this gigantic steal. Sitting Bull proved that his power over the Sioux still held when he induced everyone, even McLaughlin's yes-boys, the agent-created chiefs, Gall, John Grass, Big Head and Mad Bear, not to sign. McLaughlin was furious. His position on the reservation would be intolerable if he could not control even those he had elevated to power.

Sitting Bull soon went to Washington, heading a delegation that was to confer with the Secretary of the Interior. Some of his men begged him not to be so insolent, so over-bearing in his dealings with the Secretary.

"The only way to get along with the white man is to put on his face," he said blandly.

He succeeded in getting the price raised to $1.25 an acre. Yet when General Crook came to the agency in 1889 to complete the deal, Sitting Bull would not allow his people to sell.

McLaughlin knew that his future was at stake. If he could not get the Sioux to agree to the cession of the lands he would lose face completely with the Indians and the government as well. So the agent got hold of his own appointed chiefs, told them that rations would be sharply reduced if they did not get their people into line. Then, by his own admission, he prepared the speech John Grass was to deliver.

McLaughlin's scheme was successful. Sitting Bull and his followers were not informed of the time of the meeting. And when they did arrive their entrance was blocked by armed guards. In this way the Sioux reservation passed out of their possession forever. And McLaughlin's "face" was saved. For once he had outsmarted Sitting Bull.

CHAPTER NINETEEN

The Ghost Dance

SITTING BULL'S heart was heavy for his people. Never had he seen such utter despair settle upon their spirits. He knew that it was hard for the heart to be light when the belly was lean. But his people had faced hunger before without giving way. During lean winters when food was scarce they merely huddled in their tipis, conserved their energy and kept spirits gay with stories and songs. But now it was as if hope were dead in their hearts forever. Always before there was the knowledge that the buffalo herds would come again. Now, though, they knew that the buffalo would not return—ever. The herds were destroyed by the greedy white men. Their lands were gone—the sacred Black Hills and now the Sioux reservations—and the promise of the Commissioners to increase the rations when the lands were sold was not kept. The crops failed during the dry summer and now the Indians were gaunt with hunger and listless with despair. Life had become a burden almost too heavy to bear.

Then suddenly hope was reborn in the hearts of the natives. It was as if a wind whipped into flame the dying embers of the Indian spirit.

It all started the day of a total eclipse of the sun. The terrified Sioux, believing the sun, like the hope in their hearts, was dead, rushed out and commenced firing their guns into the sky. When the sun emerged again a moan of thanksgiving rose from their throats. They believed they had shot away the black spirit and brought the sun back to life.

On the day the "sun died," a Paiute Indian named Wovoka, living in Mason Valley in Nevada, went into the hills and had a great Vision. As he expressed it, "when the sun died I went up to heaven and saw God and all the people who had died a long time ago. God told me to come back and tell my people they must be good and love one another and not fight or steal or lie. He gave me this dance to give to my people."

It was a simple and beautiful message, certainly well in accord with Christian teachings. He came back from the hills and delivered it to his people. News of his Vision spread to other tribes, and gained embellishments in traveling. Soon messengers from far and wide came to Wovoka to hear of his revelation. There is no evidence that Wovoka ever deviated from his simple story, but the news walkers who carried the tale to the various Indian reservations each added his own personal flourish to it until by the time Short Bull and Kicking Bear brought the story to Star.ding Rock, it had become the exact answer to the prayer long in the despairing Indians' hearts, furnishing the breeze to fan hope alive once more.

According to the version reaching Sitting Bull's people, the Messiah was coming to earth again. Once He came to save the white man, but they nailed Him to a cross. This time He was coming to save His red children. The earth would rise up and tremble and the white men would be destroyed. And the buffalo herds would return and the red men would rule the world. In order to hasten the coming of the Messiah the Indians must faithfully perform the Ghost Dance. They also must wear white muslin shirts painted with moon, star and buffalo. They need fear no harm from the white man then, for the white shirts would turn away bullets.

A curious mixture of Christian and pagan religions, and it spread like wind-driven prairie to the North, South, East and West, to all over the reservations until the throb of the tom-tom echoed night and day over the plains and from hill to hill and all the Indians west of the Missouri were dancing night and day.

It was purely a religious dance and carried no military significance whatever. Similar religious frenzies among white people have swept the country from time to time. But the jittery agents and white settlers could see in the Messiah craze and its rituals nothing but a war dance.

Fear swept through the countryside. The newspapers got

hold of the story and made screaming headlines of it. The Indians were rising. There was about to be an outbreak of war. Everyone remembered Sitting Bull as the arch-criminal who slaughtered Custer's command. The chief had never become reconciled to the ways of the white man. He was stirring up trouble.

As a matter of fact, Sitting Bull had little to do with the Ghost Dance. He welcomed Short Bull and Kicking Bear and listened to their story. It is doubtful that he put much stock in it himself, but he was glad to see hope spring anew in the hearts of his people; he was glad to see them dancing in the Indian way; once again taking up the Indian beliefs.

He danced a little himself, but not much. His own heart was not in it; yet he was an interested watcher of the ceremonies. Several sweat lodges were put up to purify the young men for the dance. No ornaments were worn, only eagle feathers in the hair and the long white shirts that would turn away bullets.

The Medicine Man ran through the village calling the people, then stationed himself near the sacred tree in the center of the dance circle and commenced to chant of the vision he saw while in the trance. Then the drums began to throb and the people grasped hands and began to stamp, moving forward, backward and always to the left.

At first the movement was slow while the Medicine Man prayed to the *Wakan Tanka* to hasten the coming of the Messiah to free the red men and bring back the buffalo herds. Then he began to leap and shout; the beat of the tom-toms increased in tempo as did the stamping of the Indians in the circle until they worked themselves into a frenzy.

In vain the agents on the various reservations tried to put a stop to the Ghost Dancing. Troops were being rushed to some of the agencies. Friends brought news to Sitting Bull that he was being blamed for the craze and that McLaughlin was planning to arrest him. The chief only shrugged.

"Let McLaughlin stop the Ghost Dancing if he does not like it," he said. "I did not start it and I will not stop it. It is good to see my people dancing in the old way."

Mary Collins came to plead with Sitting Bull.

"The schools and churches are empty," she wailed. "You must put a stop to this senseless dancing."

"The red man's ways are best for the red man," he said quietly. "Let my people dance. Your people shout at prayers in your churches. The dancers are harming no one."

"Their rations will be cut off. You will be arrested," Mary Collins cried.

"If McLaughlin must find some excuse to arrest me, let this be it," the chief replied. "And my people are being slowly starved as it is."

Buffalo Bill heard about the trouble his old friend, Sitting Bull, was in and he rushed to General Miles' headquarters at Chicago and asked for permission to go and get the chief. Miles granted the permission and the showman hurried to Bismarck where he hired a livery-stable rig, loaded it with candy and presents and galloped to the reservation. There he met with an obstacle of major proportions in the unbending will of James McLaughlin who wanted to handle the matter in his own way.

"Of course you cannot bring Sitting Bull in," the agent snapped. "You would be killed before you got halfway."

"Nonsense!" cried Buffalo Bill. "Bull is my friend. He will come with me. I'm not afraid. I understand Indians."

McLaughlin was not pleased at this implication that he did not understand Indian nature. He repeated his refusal to allow Buffalo Bill to go after the chief. Then the showman drew forth the official order signed by Major General Miles, authorizing him to carry out the mission. McLaughlin reluctantly had to bow to this order from his superior officer.

However, as soon as Buffalo Bill was out of sight the agent started burning up the wires with frantic appeals to have Miles' order rescinded lest Buffalo Bill precipitate an Indian outbreak.

McLaughlin got his wish. Buffalo Bill was met by a group of Indian police who showed him the telegram countermanding Miles' order. Reluctantly he returned.

Johnny Baker, Buffalo Bill's protégé, later said, "If they had let him alone, Buffalo Bill would have captured Sitting Bull with a lollipop."

And he might have done just about that, but McLaughlin had plans of his own.

Captain Fechet, with one hundred soldiers, a cannon and forty Indian police led by Lieutenant Bull Head, and Sergeants Shave Head and Red Tomahawk, met at night at Sitting Bull's village on the Grand River. Quite a formidable force to arrest one old man! Bull Head was riding the horse Buffalo Bill had given Sitting Bull as a parting present.

It was still dark when the soldiers and Indian police swarmed into and around the little log cabin. Bull Head and Shave Head rudely seized the chief's shoulders and shook him, shouting, "We have come to arrest you. Do not fight or we will have to kill you."

Sitting Bull sat up blinking his eyes in the light of sputtering matches.

He was pulled out of bed, naked and shivering.

The police thrust articles of clothing at him trying to hustle him into them.

"Don't hurry me," he said sleepily. "What is the matter?"

Little Assiniboin, the Hóhe Sitting Bull had adopted as a boy, rushed into the cabin crying, "My brother, they have come to take you."

Crow Foot, Sitting Bull's favorite son, sat on his cot and cried, "You always said you would never let the Blue Coats take you. Now you are submitting to our own people in Blue Coats. That is worse."

The chief was fully awake now. "I am not going!" he cried.

He tried to break away from his captors and, half-clothed, reached the door of his cabin.

Bull Head grabbed his arm, then the first shot rang out and Bull Head fell, hit by Little Assiniboin. But Bull Head was not dead. He turned and fired twice, hitting Sitting Bull at close range. Red Tomahawk fired twice into the prisoner's back.

Then everyone started yelling and firing and running about. No one knew who shot whom. When it was over eight Hunkpapas besides Sitting Bull lay dead. Among them were Crow Foot, his son, and Little Assiniboin who was with his brother in death as he had been in life.

Four of the Indian police were dead, two were to die later and two more were wounded.

Sitting Bull's body was dumped into a wagon and taken to the agency where it was hurriedly buried, for some incomprehensible reason—in quicklime.

And so it was over. Sitting Bull would plague McLaughlin no more. At long last his power was broken.

CHAPTER TWENTY

The Curtain Falls

SITTING BULL was dead, but that was not the end to the Indian trouble. Not quite. The terrified Hunk-papas joined Big Foot's band and fled to the Valley of Wounded Knee. They must have known the flight would be useless but terror knows no reason.

Major Whiteside of the 7th Cavalry quickly rode the Indians down and ordered them to surrender. The command was immediately complied with. Whiteside then trained his Hotchkiss guns on the village and instructed the warriors to turn in their arms. The order produced but a few rifles. Whiteside sent his men to search the tipis.

Hereupon, Good For Nothing, the well-named nephew of Big Foot, a rattle-brained fellow, commenced to harangue his people, reminding them that they still wore their bullet-proof white ghost shirts. Why did they not resist the soldiers?

Then someone, no one knows who, fired a rifle by mistake or accident. This was excuse enough—the signal for the slaughter to commence. The Hotchkiss guns went booming up the narrow valley and the fleeing redskins, warriors, women and children, fell, their blood turning the snow-covered ground to crimson. In a short time it was over. The white ghost shirts did not stop the bullets.

It was all so needless, so futile, so utterly cruel, the slaying of Sitting Bull and the slaughter of his terrified people at Wounded Knee. But it ended for all time the strife with the Indians. They never fought the white men again. It ended, too, the Ghost Dancing. What use to dance and sing and pray for the coming of the Messiah to free them and bring back the buffalo herds? All hope was dead in the hearts of the Sioux. Their way of life was gone forever. Now they must bend their necks to the yokes of civilization. Ruthless as its progress may seem, savagery must ever give way to the march of civilization.

Life on the plains in the heyday of the Sioux was good. Sitting Bull fought valiantly and long to hold off the flood that would destroy the good way of life for his people. But civilization won out, as it always must.

Dim trails gave way to roads of steel. Where once roamed herds of shaggy buffaloes, now placid cattle graze. And where once the restless Hunkpapas pitched their tipis for a day or two are now busy towns, while the stretches that were once the Indians' battle grounds are now a vast checkerboard of farms. The "good way" of life of Sitting Bull's day is gone forever, but for a new generation of civilized, educated Indians the new way of life is good, too.

Chronology of Sitting Bull's Life and of the Sioux Country

1830-1834: Born near the Grand River. (The date of Sitting Bull's birth can be given only approximately since the Indians had no calendar corresponding to ours. The guess given by the most reliable authoritics is 1831.)

1836: The first white women, Narcissa Whitman and Eliza Spalding cross the Rocky Mountains, an event of unusual historical significance, especially as regarded the Indians.

1842: First Frémont Expedition.

1842(?): Earns his name of Sitting Bull by riding the buffalo calf.

1843(?): Sitting Bull, a boy of about twelve, counts first coup on a Crow warrior.

1843(?): The first buffalo hunt.

1845(?): The Vision Quest.
The first Sun Dance.

1845: The first caravan of settlers crosses the Plains.

1845-6: First white men on the Plains: the trappers.

1849: Fort Laramie becomes a military post.

1851: The Great Treaty Council at Fort Laramie, to gain the Indians' promise to allow roads and military posts on their lands in exchange for annuities.

1852: Sitting Bull becomes a member of the Strong Heart Warrior Society.

1854: Grattan Massacre: the first massacre on the Plains.

1859: The Pony Express.

1861: Telegraph line to California established.
Civil War takes many soldiers from frontier forts.

1863: Bozeman Road through the Sioux' Powder River hunting grounds established.

1864: Chivington (Sand Creek) Massacre in Colorado, November 29, leading to the outbreak of Indian Wars on the Plains.

1865: Powder River Expedition led by Connor.
Harney-Sanborn Treaty: Sitting Bull refuses to sign.

1866: Forts Reno and Phil Kearny built on the Bozeman Trail.
Fetterman Massacre at Fort Phil Kearny, December 21.

1867: Union Pacific Railroad built through Sioux country.
Wagon Box Fight near Fort Phil Kearny August 2.

1868: Treaty of 1868, promising the Sioux all of the Black Hills and Powder River country.

1869: The Iron Trail binds together the shores of the continent.

1874: Custer Expedition into the Black Hills leading to:

1875: The opening of the "Thieves' Road" into the Sioux' sacred Black Hills.

1876: Rosebud Battle, June 17.
Custer Massacre, June 25.
Battle of Slim Buttes, September 9.
Fight between General Miles and Sitting Bull, October 21.

1877:   Crazy Horse deserts Sitting Bull and surrenders. Sitting Bull flees with his band to Canada.

1878:   Remnants of Chief Joseph's band come to Sitting Bull's camp with plea for help.

1881:   Sitting Bull surrenders at Fort Buford, Montana, July 19. Placed under arrest. Sent to Fort Randall.

1883:   Allowed to join his own people near Standing Rock Agency.

1885:   Joins Buffalo Bill's Wild West Show.

1889:   The Ghost Dance.

1890:   Death of Sitting Bull, December 15. Battle of Wounded Knee and the end of Indian hostilities, December 28.

BIBLIOGRAPHY

Annals of Wyoming, "Sitting Bull Deals with a Rebel," October, 1929. Wyoming State Historical Society.

Bent, George to George Hyde, "Bent Letters," State Historical Society of Colorado, 1905.

Boyd, James, "Indian Wars," Publishers' Union, Philadelphia, 1891.

Brady, Cyrus Townsend, "Indian Fights and Fighters," Doubleday, Page, Garden City, N. Y., 1904.

Britt, Albert, "Great Indian Chiefs," Whittlesey House, New York, 1938.

Bulletin 61, Bureau of American Ethnology, Washington, D. C., "Teton Sioux Music."

Burt, Struthers, "Powder River," Farrar & Rinehart, New York, 1939.

Chief Luther Standing Bear, "My People the Sioux," Houghton Mifflin, New York, 1928.

Chittenden, Hiram M., and Alfred T. Richardson (edited by), "Life, Letters and Travels of Father Pierre Jean De Smet, S.J., Among the North American Indians," Harper, New York, 1905.

Chittenden, Hiram M., "The American Fur Trade of the Far West," Press of the Pioneers, New York, 1935.

Coutant, C. G., "The History of Wyoming," Chaplin, Spafford & Mathison, Laramie, Wyoming, 1899.

Crozier, Major L. E. F., "Sitting Bull's Account of Custer's Last Fight," *Canadian Historical Journal*, 1835.

Curtis, Natalie, "The Indian Book," Harper, New York, 1907.

DeBarthe, F., "The Life and Adventures of Frank Grouard," Combe Publishing Company, St. Joseph, Mo., 1894.

DeLand, Charles E., "The Sioux Wars," in South Dakota Historical Collections, Vol. XV, Department of History, Pierre, South Dakota.

Dorsey, James Owen, "Siouan Indian Religion and Mythology," U. S. Bureau of Ethnology, Washington, D. C., 11th Annual Report, 1889-90.

Eastman, Charles A., "Indian Boyhood," Little, Brown & Co., Boston, Mass., 1902.

Eastman, Charles A., "The Soul of the Indian," Houghton Mifflin, Boston, Mass., 1911.

Eastman, Charles A., "Indian Heroes and Great Chieftains," Little, Brown & Co., Boston, Mass., 1918.

Eastman, Elaine Goodale, "Pratt, the Red Man's Moses," University of Oklahoma Press, Norman, Okla., 1932.

Embree, Edwin R., "Indians of America," Houghton Mifflin, Boston, Mass., 1939.

Garst, Shannon, "Story of Wyoming," Enterprise Company, Douglas, Wyoming, 1938.

Garst, Shannon, "Custer: Fighter of the Plains," Julian Messner, Inc., New York, 1944.

Garst, Shannon, "When the West Was Young," Enterprise Co., Douglas, Wyo., 1942.

Garst, Shannon, "Kit Carson: Trail Blazer and Scout," Julian Messner, Inc., New York, 1942.

Garst, Shannon, "The Story of Buffalo Bill," Bobbs-Merrill, Indianapolis, Indiana, 1938.

Godfrey, Gen. E. S., "Custer's Last Battle," Century Magazine, January, 1892.

Hafen, LeRoy, Ph.D., Litt.D. and Francis Marion Young, A.B., "Fort Laramie and the Pageant of the West." 2 vol. The Arthur H. Clark Co., Glendale, Calif., 1938.

Hebard, Grace Raymond, "The Pathbreakers from River to Ocean," Lakeside Press, Chicago, 1913.

Johnson, Willis Fletcher, "Life of Sitting Bull," Edgewood Publishing Co., Edgewood, S. D., 1891.

Marquis, Thomas B., "A Warrior Who Fought Custer," Midwest Publishing Co., Minneapolis, Minn., 1931.

McLaughlin, James M., "My Friend the Indian," Houghton Mifflin, Boston, Mass., 1930.

Miles, Gen. Nelson A., "Personal Recollections of," Werner Co., Chicago, Ill., 1897.

Moorehead, Warren K., "The American Indian in the United States," Andover Press, Andover, Maine, 1914.

Sabin, Edwin L., "Kit Carson Days," Press of the Pioneers, New York, 1935.

Sabin, Edwin L., "Boy's Book of Indian Warriors," George W. Jacobs Co., Philadelphia, Pa., 1918.

Sandoz, Mari, "Crazy Horse," Alfred A. Knopf, Inc., New York, 1942.

Shield, Col. G. O., "The Blanket Indian of the Northwest," Vichten Waring, New York, 1921.

South Dakota Historical Collections, "Some Sidelights on the Character of Sitting Bull," Doane Robinson, Vol. 5, State Publishing Co., Pierre, S. D., 1910.

Spring, Agnes, "Caspar Collins," Columbia University Press, New York, 1927.

Superintendent of Indian Affairs, "Letter Book," Among the manuscripts of the Kansas Historical Society, Topeka, Kans.

Vestal, Stanley, "Sitting Bull," Houghton Mifflin, Boston, Mass., 1932.

Walsh, Richard J., "The Making of Buffalo Bill," A. L. Burt, New York, 1928.

Wellman, Paul I., "Death on the Prairie," The Macmillan Co., New York, 1934.

Wissler, Clark, Curator of Anthropology, "North American Indians," Lancaster Press, Lancaster, Pa., 1934.

Wissler, Clark, "Indians of the United States," Doubleday, Doran & Co., New York, 1940.

INDEX

About the Author

SHANNON GARST was born in Ironwood, Michigan, on July 24, 1899 and moved to Denver, Colorado, at the age of four, where she received most of her schooling. At the age of seventeen she went to Hood River, Oregon, where she taught school for four years. She now lives in Wyoming. Her first acceptances in the field of writing were stories she did for her own children. Since then she has become a versatile writer of juvenile fiction and biography.